ULTIMATE BAOFENG MASTERY

Essential Skills for

Emergency Communication

Maxwell Fielding

Emergency Communication Checklist
Essential Frequency List
Quick Transmission Tips
And more

CLAIM YOUR BONUS NOW

Copyright © 2024 by Maxwell Fielding

All rights reserved. No part of this publication may be reproduced, distributed, or transmitted in any form or by any means, including photocopying, recording, or other electronic or mechanical methods, without the prior written permission of the publisher, except in the case of brief quotations embodied in critical reviews and certain other noncommercial uses permitted by copyright law.

Table of Contents

INTRODUCTION 6
    OVERVIEW OF BAOFENG RADIOS 6
    IMPORTANCE OF COMMUNICATION IN EMERGENCIES 6

CHAPTER 1: **GETTING STARTED WITH YOUR BAOFENG RADIO** 8
    UNBOXING AND SETUP 8
    UNDERSTANDING THE BASIC FUNCTIONS 10
        The Keypad and Display 10
        Basic Operations 11
        Menu Navigation 12
        Common Menu Settings 12

CHAPTER 2: **PROGRAMMING YOUR BAOFENG RADIO** 14
    STEP-BY-STEP PROGRAMMING GUIDE 14
    COMMON PROGRAMMING CHALLENGES AND SOLUTIONS 17

CHAPTER 3: **ADVANCED FEATURES AND FUNCTIONS** 19
    USING ADDITIONAL FEATURES: VOX, DUAL WATCH, AND MORE 19
        Voice-Operated Exchange (VOX) 19
        Dual Watch (TDR) 21
        CTCSS/DCS Tones 22
        Repeater Access 23
        Scanning Features 25
        Priority Channel Scan 26
    CUSTOMIZING SETTINGS FOR OPTIMAL PERFORMANCE 28
        Adjusting Squelch Levels 28
        Setting Transmit Power Levels 29
        Battery Saver 29
        Timeout Timer (TOT) 30
        Wide/Narrow Band Selection 31

Backlight and Display Settings 31

Key Beep and Alert Tones 32

Channel Names and Memory Channels 33

VOX Sensitivity 34

CHAPTER 4: PRACTICAL APPLICATIONS IN EMERGENCY SITUATIONS 35

CREATING AN EFFECTIVE COMMUNICATION PLAN 36

SCENARIO-BASED GUIDES FOR EMERGENCIES 38

Natural Disasters (e.g., Earthquakes, Hurricanes, Floods) 38

Medical Emergencies 39

Search and Rescue Operations 41

Community Coordination During Power Outages 42

Coordination with Emergency Services 43

CHAPTER 5: MAINTENANCE AND TROUBLESHOOTING 45

REGULAR MAINTENANCE TIPS 45

TROUBLESHOOTING COMMON ISSUES 49

CHAPTER 6: LEGAL AND SAFETY CONSIDERATIONS 54

FCC REGULATIONS AND LEGAL USE 54

SAFETY TIPS FOR RADIO USAGE 58

CHAPTER 7: ENHANCING YOUR BAOFENG EXPERIENCE 63

RECOMMENDED ACCESSORIES 63

EXPANDING YOUR COMMUNICATION CAPABILITIES 73

CONCLUSION 83

Introduction

If you're reading this book, chances are you recognize the importance of being prepared, especially when it comes to communication. In today's world, staying connected can be a matter of life and death, particularly in emergency situations. This book is designed to help you master the use of Baofeng radios, a popular and versatile communication tool that has become a favorite among outdoor enthusiasts, preppers, and amateur radio operators.

Overview of Baofeng Radios

Baofeng radios have earned a solid reputation for their affordability, reliability, and feature-rich design. These handheld transceivers, often referred to as "HTs," are used for two-way communication and can operate on various frequency bands. Baofeng radios come in different models, with the UV-5R series being one of the most popular due to its ease of use and wide range of capabilities.

What sets Baofeng radios apart from other communication devices? Firstly, they are incredibly cost-effective. While high-end radios can be prohibitively expensive, Baofeng offers powerful radios at a fraction of the price, making them accessible to a wider audience. Secondly, they are highly customizable. With the right knowledge and tools, you can program these radios to suit your specific needs, from setting up local frequencies to optimizing performance for emergency scenarios.

Despite their advantages, Baofeng radios can seem daunting to new users. The initial setup, programming, and operation might appear complex, especially if you're not familiar with radio communication. That's where this book comes in. My goal is to break down these complexities into simple, actionable steps, ensuring you can confidently use your Baofeng radio when it matters most.

Importance of Communication in Emergencies

Communication is a critical component in any emergency situation. When disaster strikes, whether it's a natural disaster like a hurricane or earthquake, or a man-made crisis like a power outage or civil unrest, reliable communication can make all the difference. It can help coordinate rescue efforts, keep you informed about the situation, and allow you to stay in touch with family and friends.

In many emergencies, traditional forms of communication, such as cell phones and the internet, may become unreliable or completely unavailable. Cell towers can be damaged, and power outages can disrupt service for extended periods. This is where having a Baofeng radio can be a lifesaver.

Baofeng radios operate on frequencies that are less likely to be affected by infrastructure failures. They can communicate directly with other radios, bypassing the need for external networks. This direct communication capability is invaluable when traditional systems are down. With a Baofeng radio, you can reach out to others within your range, coordinate with emergency responders, and receive crucial updates.

For outdoor enthusiasts, Baofeng radios provide an added layer of safety. Whether you are hiking in remote areas, camping in the wilderness, or exploring off-the-grid locations, having a reliable means of communication is essential. In areas where cell phone coverage is sparse or non-existent, a Baofeng radio can be your lifeline.

Preppers, who prioritize readiness for any potential disaster, often include Baofeng radios in their emergency kits. These radios ensure that even in the most challenging circumstances, they can maintain communication. Preppers understand that during emergencies, being able to communicate can be the key to survival.

Amateur radio operators, or "hams," also find Baofeng radios useful for their versatility and ease of use. Ham radio enthusiasts often engage in emergency communication drills and community support efforts, where reliable radios are essential. Baofeng radios fit well into this role, providing a dependable tool for both casual use and critical situations.

This book will guide you through the essential skills needed to operate your Baofeng radio confidently and effectively. You'll learn how to set up and program your radio, optimize its performance, and use it in a variety of real-world scenarios.

By the end of this journey, you will have transformed from a novice to a proficient Baofeng radio user, ready to handle communication in any situation. Let's get started on your path to mastering Baofeng radios and ensuring you stay connected when it matters most.

Chapter 1:

Getting Started with Your Baofeng Radio

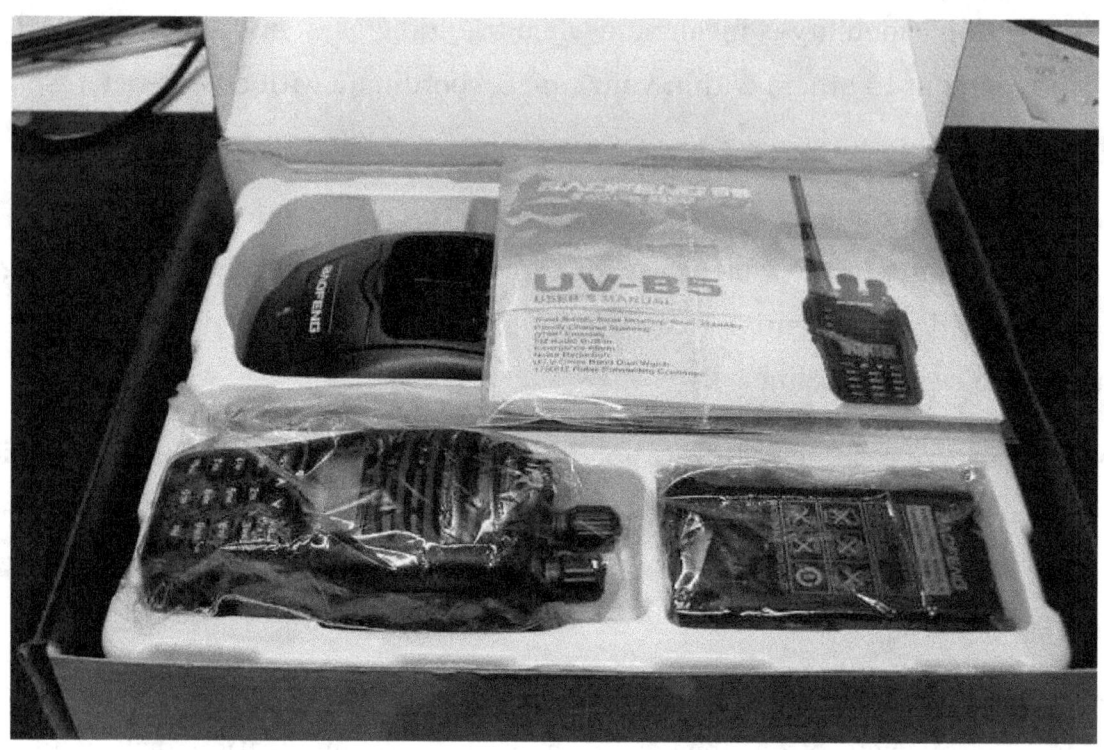

Unboxing and Setup

When you first open your Baofeng radio package, you should find the following items:

1. **Baofeng Radio Unit**: The main transceiver.
2. **Antenna**: Detachable and essential for transmitting and receiving signals.
3. **Battery Pack**: Rechargeable lithium-ion battery.
4. **Belt Clip**: Allows you to attach the radio to your belt or bag.
5. **Wrist Strap**: For easy carrying.
6. **Charger**: Base charger with AC adapter.
7. **Earpiece with Microphone**: For hands-free operation.

8. **User Manual**: Manufacturer's instructions.

Before proceeding, check that all components are included and undamaged. If anything is missing or broken, contact your seller for a replacement.

Initial Setup

Step 1: Assembling the Radio

1. **Attach the Antenna**: Take the antenna and screw it onto the top of the radio unit. Make sure it's securely fastened but avoid over-tightening.

2. **Insert the Battery Pack**: Align the battery pack with the back of the radio and slide it into place until it clicks. Ensure the contacts are properly aligned.

3. **Attach the Belt Clip (Optional)**: If you plan to use the belt clip, screw it onto the back of the radio using the provided screws and a small screwdriver.

4. **Attach the Wrist Strap (Optional)**: Loop the strap through the designated hole on the radio to secure it.

Step 2: Charging the Battery

1. **Connect the Charger**: Plug the AC adapter into the charging base and then into a wall outlet.

2. **Charge the Radio**: Place the radio into the charging base. The LED indicator on the charger will light up, usually red during charging and green when fully charged. It typically takes about 4-5 hours to fully charge a new battery. Avoid overcharging to prolong battery life.

Step 3: Turning On the Radio

1. **Power On**: Turn the knob on the top of the radio clockwise until you hear a click. This is the power/volume knob. The screen should light up, and you may hear a beep indicating the radio is powered on.

Understanding the Basic Functions

Now that you've unboxed and set up your Baofeng radio, it's time to dive deeper into understanding its basic functions. Mastering these functions is essential to using your radio effectively in any situation. In this section, we will analyze the different buttons that are available, knobs, and features of your Baofeng radio in detail.

The Keypad and Display
The front panel of your Baofeng radio includes a keypad and a display screen. Let's break down these components:

Display Screen

The display screen provides crucial information about the radio's current status and settings. Here's what you typically see on the screen:

- **Frequency Display**: Shows the current operating frequency. In dual watch mode, you'll see two frequencies.
- **Channel Number**: When in channel mode, the display shows the current channel number.
- **Battery Indicator**: Displays the remaining battery life.
- **Signal Strength Meter**: Indicates the strength of the received signal.
- **Operation Mode Icons**: Symbols that show the current mode (e.g., VFO, MR, TX power level, etc.).

Keypad

The keypad consists of numbers and several function keys. Each key serves multiple purposes, depending on the context:

- **Numeric Keys (0-9)**: Used for entering frequencies, channel numbers, and menu selections.
- ***** Key****: Often serves as a shift key to access secondary functions.
- **# Key**: Used to lock and unlock the keypad.
- **Menu Key**: Opens the menu for accessing and changing settings.
- **Exit Key**: Exits the current menu or function and returns to the main screen.
- **Arrow Keys (Up/Down)**: Scroll through menu options and adjust settings.
- **A/B Key**: Switches between the upper and lower displays (dual watch mode).
- **VFO/MR Key**: Toggles between Frequency Mode (VFO) and Memory Mode (MR).
- **PTT (Push-to-Talk) Button**: Located on the side, this button is used to transmit your voice.

Basic Operations

Understanding the basic operations of your Baofeng radio is crucial for effective communication. Let's go through some essential operations:

Turning the Radio On and Off

- **Power On**: Turn the knob on the top of the radio clockwise until you hear a click. The display will light up, and you may hear a beep indicating the radio is powered on.
- **Power Off**: Turn the knob counterclockwise until it clicks and the display turns off.

Adjusting Volume

- Turn the same knob (power/volume) clockwise to increase the volume and counterclockwise to decrease it.
- Ensure the volume is set to a comfortable level where you can hear transmissions clearly.

Selecting a Frequency

- **Direct Entry**: Use the numeric keypad to enter the desired frequency directly. Example: To set the frequency to 145.520 MHz, simply press 1-4-5-5-2-0.
- **Frequency Mode (VFO)**: If you aren't currently in Frequency Mode, you can enter it by pressing the VFO/MR key on your keyboard.

Switching Between VFO and Memory Mode

- **VFO Mode**: Allows you to manually enter and scan frequencies.

- **Memory Mode (MR)**: Accesses pre-programmed channels. Press the VFO/MR key to toggle between these modes.

Menu Navigation

Navigating the menu system of your Baofeng radio enables you to customize its settings according to your preferences and requirements. A guide to navigating the menu and adjusting the settings is as follows:

1. **Press the Menu Button**: Pressing the Menu button displays the main menu on the screen, showing a list of available menu items and options.

2. **Use Arrow Keys to Navigate**: Use the up/down arrow keys to navigate through the menu items listed on the screen. Scroll through the options until you find the setting or feature you want to adjust.

3. **Select an Option**: Once you've highlighted the desired menu item, press the Menu button again to select it. This will display the submenu or options associated with the selected item.

4. **Change Settings**: Use the numeric keypad or arrow keys to adjust the settings or select specific options within the submenu. Depending on the setting, you may need to enter numerical values, toggle between options, or enable/disable certain features.

5. **Exit Menu**: After making your changes, press the Exit button to exit the current menu and return to the main screen. Your settings will be saved, and your radio will operate according to the new configurations you've set.

Common Menu Settings

Your Baofeng radio offers a wide range of menu settings that allow you to customize its operation and performance. Here are some common menu settings you might encounter:

Here are some common settings you might need to adjust:

Squelch Level (SQL)

- **Function**: Adjusts the threshold for signal noise. Lower settings make the radio more sensitive to weak signals, while higher settings filter out background noise.
- **How to Set**: Access the SQL option in the menu, and use the arrow keys to set the desired level (0-9).

Transmit Power (TXP)

- **Function**: Switches between high and low power modes. High power is for long-distance communication, while low power conserves battery life.
- **How to Set**: Access the TXP option in the menu, and choose between HIGH and LOW.

Step Frequency (STEP)

- **Function**: Determines the increments for frequency tuning (e.g., 2.5kHz, 5kHz).
- **How to Set**: Access the STEP option in the menu, and select the desired step size.

Wide/Narrow Bandwidth (WN)

- **Function**: Sets the bandwidth for signal reception. Narrow bandwidth can reduce interference.
- **How to Set**: Access the WN option in the menu, and select WIDE or NARROW.

Channel Name (CH-NAME)

- **Function**: Allows you to name the channels for easier identification.
- **How to Set**: Access the CH-NAME option, and use the keypad to enter a name for the channel.

Chapter 2:

Programming Your Baofeng Radio

While basic operation can be performed directly on the radio, programming your Baofeng for specific frequencies and channels requires a bit more setup. This can be done manually or using software.

Step-by-Step Programming Guide

Programming your Baofeng radio can seem daunting at first, but with a systematic approach, you'll find it straightforward. Here's a step-by-step guide for both manual and software-based programming:

Manual Programming

Step 1: Enter Frequency Mode (VFO)

Press the VFO/MR button to switch to Frequency Mode if you are not already in it. This mode allows you to manually input frequencies.

Step 2: Enter the Desired Frequency

Using the numeric keypad, enter the desired frequency directly. For example, to set the frequency to 146.520 MHz, press 1-4-6-5-2-0.

Step 3: Save the Frequency to a Channel

1. Press the Menu button to access the menu options.
2. Use the up/down arrow keys to navigate to the "MEM-CH" (Memory Channel) option and press Menu to select it.
3. Use the arrow keys to choose a channel number where you want to save the frequency.
4. Press Menu to confirm the selection. You should see "Receiving Memory" on the display.
5. Press Exit to return to Frequency Mode. Your frequency is now saved to the selected channel.

Step 4: Repeat for Additional Frequencies

Repeat the above steps to program additional frequencies into other channels.

Using Software (e.g., CHIRP)

CHIRP is a free, open-source software used for programming amateur radios. It supports a wide range of radio models, including Baofeng radios, and allows users to manage and organize radio settings, frequencies, channels, and other configurations conveniently from a computer.

Features and Functionalities of CHIRP

- **Radio Compatibility:** CHIRP supports a wide range of radio models, including multiple versions of Baofeng radios such as the UV-5R series, BF-F8HP, and many others. Its compatibility with various radio brands and models makes it a versatile tool for radio enthusiasts.
- **User-Friendly Interface:** The software offers an intuitive and easy-to-navigate interface, enabling users, including beginners, to program and manage their radios without extensive technical knowledge. The interface layout organizes functions logically, making it accessible for users to perform programming tasks efficiently.

- **Programming Capabilities:** CHIRP allows users to program a plethora of radio settings, including frequencies, channel names, squelch levels, transmit power levels, duplex settings, and much more. It simplifies the process of inputting and organizing these settings, making radio programming accessible to a wider audience.
- **Bulk Editing and Cloning:** One of CHIRP's significant advantages is its ability to perform bulk editing of channels and settings. Users can create, modify, or clone multiple channels simultaneously, enhancing efficiency when programming a large number of frequencies or radios with similar configurations.
- **Importing and Exporting Data:** CSV files are among the formats that may be imported and exported with the help of this software, which also supports other formats. This feature allows users to manage frequencies and channel lists outside the software and import them into CHIRP, streamlining the programming process.
- **Cross-Platform Compatibility:** CHIRP is compatible with a variety of operating systems, consisting of Windows, macOS, and Linux variants, among others. The availability of this cross-platform functionality means that customers can utilize it regardless of the operating environment they are using.

Step 1: Install and Open CHIRP Software

Download and install the CHIRP software from the official website (https://chirp.danplanet.com/). Once installed, open the CHIRP application on your computer.

Step 2: Connect Your Baofeng Radio

To connect your Baofeng radio to your computer, use a programming cable. It is imperative that the cable be securely inserted into the USB port of the computer as well as the radio as well.

Step 3: Download Radio Settings

In the CHIRP software, select the "Radio" menu and choose "Download From Radio." Follow the on-screen prompts to download the current settings from your Baofeng radio to the CHIRP application.

Step 4: Program Frequencies

1. In the CHIRP interface, you'll see a list of channels or frequencies.
2. Enter the desired frequencies, names, and other details for each channel.
3. Save your changes in CHIRP.

Step 5: Upload Settings to Radio

Once you've finished programming the frequencies, select the "Radio" menu and choose "Upload To Radio." Follow the on-screen prompts to upload the settings from CHIRP to your Baofeng radio.

Step 6: Disconnect and Test

After uploading the settings, disconnect the programming cable from your radio and computer. Test the programmed frequencies to ensure they are working correctly.

Common Programming Challenges and Solutions

While programming your Baofeng radio, you may encounter some common challenges. Here are solutions to help you overcome them:

1. **Incorrect Frequency Entry**

Challenge: Accidentally entering the wrong frequency can result in communication errors.

Solution: Double-check the frequency entry before saving it to a channel. Use the arrow keys to navigate and correct any mistakes.

2. **Repeater Offset and Access Tones**

Challenge: Programming repeater frequencies requires setting the correct offset and access tones (CTCSS or DCS).

Solution: Refer to repeater directories or websites to obtain the required offset and access tones. Input these values accurately when programming repeater frequencies.

3. **Limited Memory Channels**

Challenge: Baofeng radios have a limited number of memory channels, which can be insufficient for storing all desired frequencies.

Solution: Prioritize channels based on frequency of use or importance. Delete or overwrite less critical channels to make room for new ones.

4. **Compatibility Issues with Software**

Challenge: Some users may encounter compatibility issues when using programming software like CHIRP.

Solution: Ensure you are using the correct version of the software compatible with your Baofeng radio model. Check for updates or patches to resolve compatibility issues.

5. **Programming Cable Connection Problems**

Challenge: Poor connection between the programming cable and radio/computer can disrupt the programming process.

Solution: Ensure the programming cable is securely connected to both the radio and computer. Check for any loose connections or damaged cables.

6. **Confusion with Menu Navigation**

Challenge: Navigating the radio's menu system can be confusing for new users, leading to frustration.

Solution: Refer to the user manual or online guides for detailed instructions on menu navigation. Take your time to familiarize yourself with the menu structure and functions.

7. **Difficulty with Repeater Programming**

Challenge: Programming repeater frequencies and settings can be challenging for novice users.

Solution: Seek assistance from experienced users or consult online resources for step-by-step guides on repeater programming. Practice programming repeater frequencies until you feel comfortable with the process.

Chapter 3:

Advanced Features and Functions

Y ou've mastered the basics of your Baofeng radio, and you've learned how to program it for specific frequencies and channels. Now it's time to delve into the advanced features and functions that can enhance your communication capabilities.

Using Additional Features: VOX, Dual Watch, and More

Voice-Operated Exchange (VOX)
Voice-Operated Exchange (VOX) is a feature that enables hands-free operation of your Baofeng radio. Instead of manually pressing the Push-to-Talk (PTT) button to transmit, VOX automatically activates the transmission when it detects your voice. This feature offers several benefits:

1. **Hands-Free Operation**: VVOX functionality enables hands-free communication, eliminating the need to press buttons and allowing you to focus on other tasks. This proves especially valuable in scenarios where manual operation is inconvenient or impractical, such as while driving or engaging in hands-on work.

2. **Increased Convenience**: With VOX, you can initiate transmissions simply by speaking, eliminating the need to reach for the PTT button. This convenience can streamline

communication, especially in fast-paced environments where quick response times are crucial.

3. **Improved Safety**: In situations where your hands are occupied or where using a radio may be unsafe, such as during outdoor activities or emergencies, VOX ensures that you can communicate without compromising safety.

How to Set Up and Use VOX:

Setting up VOX on your Baofeng radio is a straightforward process. Follow these steps to enable VOX functionality:

Step 1: Access the Menu

- Press the Menu key on your Baofeng radio to access the menu settings.

Step 2: Navigate to VOX Option

- Use the arrow keys to navigate through the menu options until you find the VOX setting. This setting is typically located within the radio's menu options and may be labeled as "VOX" or "Voice Activation."

Step 3: Enable VOX

- Once you've located the VOX setting, press the Menu key to select it. Then, use the arrow keys to toggle the VOX setting to "ON." Press the Menu key again to confirm your selection.

Step 4: Adjust VOX Sensitivity (Optional)

- Some Baofeng radios allow you to adjust the sensitivity of the VOX feature to ensure it activates reliably based on your voice input. If your radio offers this option, navigate to the VOX sensitivity setting and adjust it according to your preferences.

Step 5: Test VOX Functionality

- After enabling VOX, perform a test to ensure that the feature is functioning correctly. Speak into the microphone of the radio at various volumes to determine the threshold at which VOX activates transmission.

Once VOX is enabled and configured to your liking, you can begin using it during communication. Simply speak into the microphone of the radio, and VOX will automatically activate transmission when it detects your voice. Be mindful of background noise and adjust the VOX sensitivity as needed to minimize false activations.

Dual Watch (TDR)

Dual Watch, also known as TDR (Dual Standby), is a feature that allows you to monitor two frequencies simultaneously on your Baofeng radio. This feature offers several benefits:

1. **Enhanced Monitoring**: With Dual Watch, you can monitor two different frequencies or channels at the same time, ensuring that you don't miss any important communications on either channel.

2. **Increased Flexibility**: Dual Watch provides added flexibility by allowing you to monitor a primary frequency while simultaneously listening to a secondary frequency. This is particularly useful in scenarios where you need to monitor multiple channels for incoming transmissions.

3. **Efficient Communication**: By monitoring two frequencies simultaneously, you can efficiently manage communication across different channels or with multiple parties, improving overall communication efficiency.

How to Set Up and Use Dual Watch:

Enabling Dual Watch on your Baofeng radio is a simple process. Follow these steps to activate Dual Watch functionality:

Step 1: Access the Menu

- Press the Menu key on your Baofeng radio to access the menu settings.

Step 2: Navigate to Dual Watch Option

- Use the arrow keys to navigate through the menu options until you find the Dual Watch setting. This setting is typically located within the radio's menu options and may be labeled as "Dual Watch" or "TDR."

Step 3: Enable Dual Watch

- Once you've located the Dual Watch setting, press the Menu key to select it. Then, use the arrow keys to toggle the Dual Watch setting to "ON." Press the Menu key again to confirm your selection.

Step 4: Select Primary and Secondary Frequencies

- After enabling Dual Watch, you'll need to select the primary and secondary frequencies that you want to monitor simultaneously. Use the A/B key on your Baofeng radio to switch between the primary (A) and secondary (B) frequencies.

Step 5: Monitor Both Frequencies

- With Dual Watch activated and the primary and secondary frequencies selected, your Baofeng radio will monitor both frequencies simultaneously. Incoming transmissions on either frequency will be received and displayed accordingly.

Once Dual Watch is enabled and configured with the desired frequencies, you can begin monitoring both channels simultaneously. Use the A/B key to switch between the primary and secondary frequencies as needed to manage communication effectively.

CTCSS/DCS Tones

Continuous Tone-Coded Squelch System (CTCSS) and Digital-Coded Squelch (DCS) tones are encoding methods used to filter out unwanted transmissions and improve signal clarity in two-way radio communication. These tones offer several benefits:

1. **Reduced Interference**: CTCSS and DCS tones help reduce interference from other users or radio signals operating on the same frequency. By filtering out transmissions that do not match the programmed tone, users can maintain clear and uninterrupted communication.

2. **Enhanced Privacy**: CTCSS and DCS tones provide a level of privacy by ensuring that only users with the correct tone settings can access and communicate on a specific channel. This is particularly useful in environments where confidentiality or security is a concern.

3. **Improved Signal Clarity**: By employing CTCSS and DCS tones, users can enhance signal clarity and minimize the impact of background noise or weak signals. This results in clearer and more reliable communication, even in challenging RF environments.

How to Set Up and Use CTCSS/DCS Tones:

Setting up CTCSS/DCS tones on your Baofeng radio involves configuring both the transmit (T-CTCSS/T-DCS) and receive (R-CTCSS/R-DCS) tones for each channel. Here's how to set up and use CTCSS/DCS tones:

Step 1: Access the Menu

- Press the Menu key on your Baofeng radio to access the menu settings.

Step 2: Navigate to CTCSS/DCS Options

- Use the arrow keys to navigate through the menu options until you find the CTCSS/DCS setting. This setting is typically located within the radio's menu options and may be labeled as "T-CTCS," "R-CTCS," "T-DCS," or "R-DCS."

Step 3: Set Transmit and Receive Tones

- Once you've located the CTCSS/DCS setting, press the Menu key to select it. Then, use the arrow keys to choose the desired tone frequency/code for both transmit and receive functions. Repeat this process for each channel that requires CTCSS/DCS tones.

Step 4: Enable CTCSS/DCS

- After setting the tones, ensure that the CTCSS/DCS function is enabled for both transmit and receive operations. This can typically be done within the same menu option by toggling the setting to "ON."

Step 5: Test Communication

- Once CTCSS/DCS tones are configured, perform a test communication to ensure that the tones are functioning correctly. Verify that communication is clear and that unwanted transmissions are filtered out.

Repeater Access
Repeater access is a crucial feature that allows users to extend their communication range by accessing repeater systems. Repeaters receive transmissions on one frequency and retransmit them on another frequency, often at a higher power and elevation, thereby extending the range of communication. Here are some benefits of repeater access:

1. **Extended Communication Range**: By accessing repeater systems, users can significantly extend their communication range, allowing them to communicate over much greater distances than would be possible with direct line-of-sight communication.

2. **Improved Signal Quality**: Repeater systems typically operate at higher power levels and are strategically located to provide optimal coverage. As a result, transmissions relayed through repeaters often experience improved signal quality and reliability compared to direct communication.

3. **Enhanced Coverage in Remote Areas**: In remote or mountainous areas where direct communication may be limited by terrain or obstacles, repeaters provide a reliable means of maintaining communication over long distances, bridging gaps in coverage.

How to Set Up and Use Repeater Access:

Setting up repeater access on your Baofeng radio involves programming the repeater's input and output frequencies, as well as any required CTCSS/DCS tones. Here's how to set up and use repeater access:

Step 1: Determine Repeater Frequencies

- Obtain the input and output frequencies of the repeater you wish to access. This information is typically available from repeater directories or online resources.

Step 2: Access the Menu

- Press the Menu key on your Baofeng radio to access the menu settings.

Step 3: Set Repeater Input Frequency

- Navigate to the menu option for setting the transmit (input) frequency of the repeater. Enter the repeater's input frequency using the keypad.

Step 4: Set Repeater Offset

- Configure the offset direction (positive or negative) and offset frequency for the repeater. This ensures that your radio transmits on the correct frequency to access the repeater.

Step 5: Set CTCSS/DCS Tones (If Required)

- If the repeater requires CTCSS/DCS tones for access, configure the transmit and receive tones accordingly using the menu settings.

Step 6: Save Repeater Settings

- Once all settings are configured, save the repeater settings to a memory channel on your Baofeng radio for easy access in the future.

Step 7: Access Repeater

- To access the repeater, simply tune your Baofeng radio to the memory channel where the repeater settings are stored, and initiate communication as usual. Your radio will automatically transmit on the repeater's input frequency with the configured offset and tones.

Scanning Features

Baofeng radios are equipped with scanning features that allow users to automatically search for and monitor active frequencies or channels. Scanning features offer several benefits:

1. **Efficient Channel Monitoring**: Scanning features enable users to efficiently monitor multiple frequencies or channels without the need for manual tuning. This allows users to stay informed of activity on various channels without constantly switching between them.

2. **Quick Identification of Active Channels**: Scanning features rapidly scan through programmed channels and stop on active frequencies, allowing users to quickly identify and respond to incoming transmissions.

3. **Enhanced Situational Awareness**: By continuously scanning for activity across multiple channels, users can maintain a high level of situational awareness and stay informed of relevant communications in their vicinity.

How to Set Up and Use Scanning Features:

Baofeng radios typically offer various scanning modes and options that can be customized to suit the user's preferences. Here's how to set up and use scanning features on your Baofeng radio:

Step 1: Access the Menu

- Press the Menu key on your Baofeng radio to access the menu settings.

Step 2: Navigate to Scanning Options

- Use the arrow keys to navigate through the menu options until you find the scanning settings. This setting may be labeled as "Scan," "Scanning," or "Scan Mode."

Step 3: Select Scanning Mode

- Choose the scanning mode that best suits your needs. Baofeng radios typically offer several scanning modes, including:
    - **Frequency Scan**: Scans through a range of frequencies to identify active channels.
    - **Channel Scan**: Scans through programmed memory channels to identify active frequencies.
    - **Priority Channel Scan**: Prioritizes specific channels during scanning.

Step 4: Set Scan Parameters

- Configure additional scan parameters as needed, such as scan direction (up, down, or both), scan resume method, and scan delay.

Step 5: Start Scanning

- Once scanning parameters are configured, initiate scanning by pressing the Scan key or activating the scanning function from the menu. The radio will begin scanning through the programmed channels or frequencies.

Step 6: Monitor Scanning Activity

- Monitor the scanning activity displayed on the radio's screen. The radio will stop scanning and display any active channels or frequencies it detects.

Step 7: Respond to Active Channels

- When the radio identifies an active channel or frequency, you can respond to incoming transmissions as needed. Simply switch to the active channel or frequency and initiate communication.

Step 8: Adjust Scan Settings (Optional)

- Depending on your preferences and scanning environment, you may need to adjust scan settings such as scan speed, scan resume method, and scan delay. Experiment with different settings to optimize scanning performance.

Priority Channel Scan

Priority channel scan is a useful feature that allows users to prioritize specific channels during scanning. This ensures that critical channels are monitored more frequently, allowing users to stay informed of important communications. Here are some benefits of priority channel scan:

1. **Focused Monitoring**: Priority channel scan enables users to focus their scanning efforts on specific channels that are deemed critical or high-priority. This ensures that important communications are not missed amidst other less critical activity.

2. **Quick Response Time**: By prioritizing specific channels, users can reduce the time it takes to identify and respond to incoming transmissions on those channels. This enhances response times and facilitates quicker decision-making in critical situations.

3. **Enhanced Situational Awareness**: Priority channel scan helps maintain a high level of situational awareness by ensuring that users are promptly alerted to important

communications as they occur. This allows for better coordination and response to changing circumstances.

How to Set Up and Use Priority Channel Scan:

Setting up priority channel scan on your Baofeng radio involves programming specific channels to be prioritized during scanning. Here's how to set up and use priority channel scan:

Step 1: Access the Menu

- Press the Menu key on your Baofeng radio to access the menu settings.

Step 2: Navigate to Priority Channel Scan Option

- Use the arrow keys to navigate through the menu options until you find the priority channel scan settings. This setting may be labeled as "Priority Scan" or "Priority Channel."

Step 3: Select Priority Channels

- Choose the channels that you want to prioritize during scanning. These channels are typically programmed into the radio's memory channels beforehand.

Step 4: Enable Priority Channel Scan

- Once the priority channels are selected, enable the priority channel scan function. This can usually be done within the same menu option by toggling the setting to "ON."

Step 5: Start Scanning

- Initiate scanning as usual. The radio will now prioritize the selected channels during scanning, ensuring that they are monitored more frequently than other channels.

Step 6: Monitor Priority Channel Activity

- Monitor the scanning activity displayed on the radio's screen. The radio will stop scanning and display any activity detected on the priority channels.

Step 7: Respond to Priority Channel Activity

- When the radio identifies activity on a priority channel, you can respond to incoming transmissions as needed. Switch to the priority channel and initiate communication as required.

Step 8: Adjust Priority Channel Settings (Optional)

- Depending on your preferences and scanning requirements, you may need to adjust priority channel settings such as scan speed and priority channel selection. Experiment with different settings to optimize scanning performance.

By leveraging these additional advanced features offered by Baofeng radios, you can significantly enhance your communication capabilities and adapt to a wide range of communication scenarios with confidence.

Customizing Settings for Optimal Performance

Optimizing your Baofeng radio involves fine-tuning various settings to match your specific needs and environment. Here, we will explore how to customize settings for the best performance.

Adjusting Squelch Levels

Squelch is a circuit in a radio receiver that mutes the audio output when the signal strength is below a certain threshold, preventing background noise from being heard. Adjusting the squelch level can help manage noise and weak signal reception.

Benefits:

1. **Noise Reduction**: Increasing the squelch level filters out weaker signals and background noise, resulting in clearer audio reception.

2. **Improved Signal Clarity**: By setting an appropriate squelch level, you can ensure that only strong, relevant signals are heard, reducing interference and improving overall signal clarity.

Setting Squelch Level

1. **Enter the Menu**: Press the Menu key.

2. **Navigate to Squelch Setting**: Use the up/down arrow keys to find "SQL" (Menu 0).

3. **Adjust Squelch Level**: Press the Menu key to select, then use the arrow keys to set the squelch level from 0 (open) to 9 (tight).

4. **Exit the Menu**: Press the Exit key to return to the main screen.

Optimal Squelch Levels

- **Level 1-3**: Suitable for noisy environments or when weak signals are expected.
- **Level 4-6**: General use, balancing sensitivity and noise suppression.
- **Level 7-9**: For very quiet environments where only strong signals are desired.

Setting Transmit Power Levels

Transmit power refers to the strength of the radio signal transmitted by your Baofeng radio. Adjusting transmit power can help conserve battery life or extend communication range, depending on your requirements.

Benefits:

1. **Extended Communication Range**: Increasing transmit power can extend the range of your radio's signal, allowing you to communicate over greater distances, especially in open areas with minimal obstructions.

2. **Conserved Battery Life**: Lowering transmit power reduces the amount of energy consumed during transmission, resulting in longer battery life. This comes in especially handy in circumstances when there is a restricted availability of power sources for the purpose of recharging.

Setting Transmit Power

1. **Enter the Menu**: Press the Menu key.

2. **Navigate to Transmit Power Setting**: Use the up/down arrow keys to find "TXP" (Menu 2).

3. **Select Power Level**: Press the Menu key to select, then use the arrow keys to choose between HIGH (high power) and LOW (low power).

4. **Exit the Menu**: Press the Exit key to return to the main screen.

Choosing the Right Power Level

- **HIGH**: Use high power for long-distance communication or when signal strength is a concern.
- **LOW**: Use low power for close-range communication to conserve battery life.

Battery Saver

The battery saver function helps to preserve the life of the battery by lowering the amount of power that is consumed by the radio while it is not in use. Enabling the battery saver can extend the operating time of your Baofeng radio, especially during periods of inactivity.

Benefits:

1. **Extended Battery Life**: By reducing power consumption during idle periods, the battery saver feature extends the operating time of the radio on a single battery charge.

2. **Increased Reliability**: With longer battery life, your Baofeng radio remains operational for extended periods, ensuring reliable communication when needed.

3. **How to Enable Battery Saver:**

4. **Access the Menu**: Press the Menu key on your Baofeng radio to access the menu settings.

5. **Navigate to SAVE Option**: Use the arrow keys to navigate to the SAVE (Battery Saver) option in the menu settings.

6. **Enable Battery Saver**: Toggle the battery saver option to "ON" to activate the feature.

7. **Adjust Settings (Optional)**: Some Baofeng radios may allow you to adjust the sensitivity or activation threshold of the battery saver. If available, customize these settings according to your preferences.

8. **Save Settings**: Once you've enabled the battery saver and made any necessary adjustments, save the settings to apply the changes.

Timeout Timer (TOT)
The timeout timer limits the duration of continuous transmission to prevent overheating and protect the radio from damage. Adjusting the timeout timer duration ensures compliance with regulatory requirements and promotes responsible radio usage.

Benefits:

1. **Prevents Overheating**: By limiting the duration of continuous transmission, the timeout timer prevents the radio from overheating, ensuring long-term reliability and durability.

2. **Compliance with Regulations**: Many regulatory bodies impose limits on the maximum duration of continuous transmission. Adjusting the timeout timer helps ensure compliance with these regulations.

How to Adjust Timeout Timer:

1. **Access the Menu**: Press the Menu key on your Baofeng radio to access the menu settings.

2. **Navigate to TOT Option**: Use the arrow keys to navigate to the TOT (Timeout Timer) option in the menu settings.

3. **Set Timer Duration**: Choose the desired duration for the timeout timer using the menu options. This duration typically ranges from a few seconds to several minutes.

4. **Save Settings**: Once you've set the timeout timer duration, save the settings to apply the changes.

Wide/Narrow Band Selection
Baofeng radios often offer the option to switch between wideband (25 kHz) and narrowband (12.5 kHz) transmission modes. Wideband mode allows for higher audio fidelity but occupies more bandwidth, while narrowband mode conserves bandwidth but may sacrifice audio quality.

Benefits:

1. **Compatibility**: Selecting the appropriate bandwidth mode ensures compatibility with the frequency band and channel spacing requirements specified by regulatory authorities or operating environments.

2. **Optimized Spectrum Usage**: Narrowband mode conserves spectrum bandwidth, making it suitable for crowded frequency bands or environments where spectrum efficiency is critical.

How to Switch Between Wide and Narrow Band:

1. **Access the Menu**: Press the Menu key on your Baofeng radio to access the menu settings.

2. **Navigate to Wide/Narrow Band Option**: Use the arrow keys to navigate to the Wide/Narrow Band option in the menu settings.

3. **Select Bandwidth Mode**: Choose the desired bandwidth mode (Wide or Narrow) based on your operational requirements and regulatory compliance.

4. **Save Settings**: Once you've selected the bandwidth mode, save the settings to apply the changes.

Backlight and Display Settings
Customizing backlight and display settings allows you to optimize visibility and conserve battery power based on your preferences and operating conditions.

Benefits:

1. **Enhanced Visibility**: Adjusting backlight intensity and display contrast improves screen readability in various lighting conditions, ensuring that information is easily visible at all times.

2. **Battery Conservation**: Dimming or disabling the backlight when not needed helps conserve battery power, extending the operating time of your Baofeng radio.

How to Customize Backlight and Display Settings:

1. **Access the Menu**: Press the Menu key on your Baofeng radio to access the menu settings.

2. **Navigate to Display Options**: Use the arrow keys to navigate to the Display options in the menu settings.

3. **Adjust Backlight Intensity**: Choose the desired backlight intensity level or timeout duration for the display.

4. **Set Display Contrast**: Adjust the display contrast to optimize screen readability.

5. **Save Settings**: Once you've customized the backlight and display settings, save the changes to apply them.

Key Beep and Alert Tones
Customizing key beep and alert tones allows you to personalize the auditory feedback provided by your Baofeng radio, enhancing user experience and operational awareness.

Benefits:

1. **Personalization**: Selecting preferred key beep and alert tones allows users to personalize their Baofeng radio to suit their preferences and operating environment.

2. **Auditory Feedback**: Key beep tones provide confirmation feedback for button presses, while alert tones notify users of important events or incoming transmissions.

How to Customize Key Beep and Alert Tones:

1. **Access the Menu**: Press the Menu key on your Baofeng radio to access the menu settings.

2. **Navigate to Tone Options**: Use the arrow keys to navigate to the Tone options in the menu settings.

3. **Adjust Key Beep Tone**: Choose the desired key beep tone or disable it altogether, depending on your preference.

4. **Set Alert Tones**: Configure alert tones for specific events such as channel activity, low battery, or signal reception.

5. **Save Settings**: Once you've customized the key beep and alert tones, save the changes to apply them.

Channel Names and Memory Channels

Customizing channel names and organizing memory channels allows for easy navigation and quick access to frequently used frequencies or channels. By assigning descriptive names and organizing channels into logical groups, you can streamline communication and improve efficiency.

Benefits:

1. **Easy Navigation**: Assigning descriptive names to channels makes it easier to identify and select the desired frequency or channel quickly, reducing the time spent searching through memory channels.

2. **Logical Organization**: Organizing memory channels into groups based on usage (e.g., local repeaters, emergency channels, favorite frequencies) facilitates efficient communication and ensures that important channels are readily accessible.

How to Customize Channel Names and Memory Channels:

1. **Access the Menu**: Press the Menu key on your Baofeng radio to access the menu settings.

2. **Navigate to Channel Edit Options**: Use the arrow keys to navigate to the Channel Edit or Memory Channel options in the menu settings.

3. **Edit Channel Names**: Select the desired memory channel and edit its name to a descriptive label using the alphanumeric keypad.

4. **Organize Memory Channels**: Group memory channels into logical categories based on usage (e.g., local channels, emergency channels, favorite frequencies) for easy navigation.

5. **Save Settings**: Once you've customized channel names and organized memory channels, save the changes to apply them.

Naming Tips

- Use abbreviations to fit the limited character space.
- Choose names that clearly indicate the channel's purpose or frequency.

VOX Sensitivity

Adjusting VOX (Voice-Operated Exchange) sensitivity allows for hands-free operation of your Baofeng radio by automatically activating transmission when it detects your voice. By fine-tuning VOX sensitivity, you can ensure reliable voice activation while minimizing false triggers.

Benefits:

1. **Hands-Free Operation**: VOX sensitivity adjustment ensures reliable hands-free operation by activating transmission only when your voice is detected, freeing up your hands for other tasks.

2. **Minimized False Triggers**: Fine-tuning VOX sensitivity reduces the likelihood of false triggers caused by background noise or ambient sounds, ensuring that transmission is initiated only when intended.

How to Adjust VOX Sensitivity:

1. **Access the Menu**: Press the Menu key on your Baofeng radio to access the menu settings.

2. **Navigate to VOX Options**: Use the arrow keys to navigate to the VOX (Voice-Operated Exchange) options in the menu settings.

3. **Adjust Sensitivity**: Select the VOX sensitivity setting and adjust it to the desired level using the menu options. Test the sensitivity level by speaking into the microphone to ensure reliable voice activation.

4. **Save Settings**: Once you've adjusted VOX sensitivity to your preference, save the changes to apply them.

Chapter 4:

Practical Applications in Emergency Situations

When it comes to emergency situations, effective communication can be the difference between safety and disaster. Baofeng radios are a versatile tool that can be used in various emergency scenarios to ensure that you and your team remain connected and informed. This chapter will guide you through creating an effective communication plan and provide scenario-based guides to help you utilize your Baofeng radio in different emergencies.

Creating an Effective Communication Plan

A well-thought-out communication plan ensures that all parties involved in an emergency know how to use their radios effectively and understand the protocols for communication. Here's how to create a robust communication plan:

1. **Assess Communication Needs**

The first step in creating a communication plan is to assess the specific communication needs of your situation. This involves considering various factors that will impact communication effectiveness, including the number of participants, the geographical area that needs coverage, available frequencies and channels, and potential sources of interference.

Factors to Consider:

- **Number of Participants**: Determine the number of individuals who will need to communicate during the emergency. This includes not only primary responders but also support staff, volunteers, and other relevant parties.
- **Geographical Area**: Evaluate the size and layout of the area that needs communication coverage. Consider whether communication will be required across long distances, in urban or rural environments, or in areas with challenging terrain.
- **Frequency Availability**: Identify the frequencies and channels available for communication. This may include frequencies allocated for emergency services, amateur radio bands, or other licensed frequencies.
- **Potential Interference**: Be aware of potential sources of interference that could disrupt communication, such as nearby radio towers, electronic devices, or natural obstacles like mountains or buildings.

2. **Choose Appropriate Frequencies**

Once you have assessed the communication needs of your situation, the next step is to choose appropriate frequencies and channels for communication. This involves selecting frequencies that provide the necessary coverage and are compatible with your equipment and regulatory requirements.

Considerations When Choosing Frequencies:

- **Primary and Secondary Channels**: Establish primary and secondary channels for communication. The primary channel should be designated for main communication, while the secondary channel serves as a backup in case of interference or congestion.

- **Emergency Channels**: Designate specific channels for emergency use. These channels should be reserved for critical communication during emergencies and should be clearly identified in the communication plan.
- **Channel Naming**: Use descriptive names for channels to facilitate easy identification and selection. Avoid generic labels and ensure that each channel serves a distinct purpose, such as command and control, logistics, or medical.

3. **Establish Communication Protocols**

Clear communication protocols are essential for ensuring that messages are understood and acted upon promptly. Communication protocols outline the procedures for initiating and conducting communication, including the format of messages, frequency of communication, and channels to be used.

Key Components of Communication Protocols:

- **Check-Ins**: Establish regular check-in procedures to confirm the status and location of all participants. Check-ins should be scheduled at predetermined intervals and should include reporting requirements for key information, such as current position, health status, and resource availability.
- **Code Words**: Define a set of predefined code words or phrases to convey specific messages quickly and efficiently. Code words can be used to communicate common messages, such as requesting assistance, signaling danger, or confirming receipt of instructions. For example, "Code Red" could indicate immediate danger, while "All Clear" signals that the situation is safe.
- **Message Format**: Standardize the format for sending messages to ensure clarity and completeness. Common message formats include the "Who, What, Where, When" format, which provides essential information in a concise and structured manner.

4. **Train Participants**

Training participants in the use of communication equipment and protocols is essential for ensuring effective communication during emergencies. Proper training ensures that all individuals understand how to operate the equipment, adhere to communication protocols, and respond appropriately to various situations.

Components of Participant Training:

- **Radio Operation**: Train participants in the basic operation of communication equipment, including turning the radio on and off, selecting channels, adjusting volume and squelch settings, and initiating transmissions.
- **Communication Etiquette**: Educate participants on proper radio etiquette, including waiting for a clear channel before transmitting, speaking clearly and concisely, using standardized language and codes, and acknowledging receipt of messages.
- **Emergency Procedures**: Conduct drills and simulations to familiarize participants with emergency procedures, such as reporting emergencies, requesting assistance, and responding to instructions from authorities.

5. **Regularly Review and Update the Plan**

A communication strategy ought to be examined and modified on a regular basis in order to guarantee that it continues to be efficient and appropriately adapted to the ever-evolving requirements and conditions of the situation. Regular reviews allow for the identification of any issues or areas for improvement and facilitate the incorporation of new information or changes in protocols.

Steps for Review and Update:

- **Feedback**: Gather feedback from participants on their experiences with the communication plan. Encourage participants to provide input on what worked well and what could be improved.
- **Drills**: Conduct regular drills and exercises to test the effectiveness of the communication plan in simulated emergency scenarios. Use drills to identify any weaknesses or gaps in communication and address them promptly.
- **Updates**: Revise the communication plan as needed based on feedback, drill outcomes, or changes in the operational environment. Ensure that all participants are informed of any updates or changes to the plan.

Scenario-Based Guides for Emergencies

To effectively use your Baofeng radio during emergencies, it's essential to understand how to apply your communication plan in different scenarios. Below are detailed guides for various emergency situations:

Natural Disasters (e.g., Earthquakes, Hurricanes, Floods)
Scenario: A major earthquake has struck your area, causing widespread damage and disruption. Communication infrastructure may be compromised, and access to emergency services may be limited.

Objective: Maintain contact with family members, coordinate evacuation or shelter-in-place actions, and provide updates on the situation.

Communication Plan:

1. Establish a designated emergency channel for family communication.
2. Compile a list of emergency contacts and frequency/channel information.
3. Designate roles and responsibilities within the family/group.

Steps:

1. **Initiate Contact:**
    - Use the designated emergency channel to check in with family members and ensure everyone is safe.
    - Communicate your location and status to each contact on your list.

2. **Coordinate Actions:**
    - Follow the pre-established evacuation plan if necessary. Use the radio to provide updates on your progress and any changes in the situation.
    - If sheltering in place, monitor local emergency channels for updates and follow instructions from authorities.

3. **Monitor Emergency Channels:**
    - Continuously monitor local emergency channels for updates and instructions from authorities.
    - Relay important information to all members of your group.

4. **Provide Assistance:**
    - Use the radio to offer assistance to neighbors or others in need, if safe to do so.
    - Coordinate efforts with local emergency services if necessary.

5. **Report Status:**
    - Regularly report your status and any changes in your situation to designated contacts.
    - Use the radio to keep everyone informed and maintain morale.

Medical Emergencies
Scenario: A member of your group has suffered a medical emergency, such as a severe allergic reaction or injury, and requires urgent assistance.

Objective: Quickly communicate with emergency medical services, coordinate care for the affected individual, and provide updates on their condition.

Communication Plan:

1. Establish contact with local emergency services on designated emergency channels.
2. Assign roles for providing first aid, contacting medical services, and relaying information to family members.

Steps:

1. **Assess the Situation:**
   - Quickly assess the medical emergency and determine the level of care needed.
   - Designate someone to provide immediate first aid while others contact emergency services.

2. **Initiate Emergency Contact:**
   - Use the designated emergency channel to contact emergency medical services and provide details of the situation.
   - Provide clear and concise information about the patient's condition and location.

3. **Coordinate with Responders:**
   - Follow instructions from EMS personnel and provide updates on the patient's condition.
   - If instructed, administer basic first aid as guided by EMS.

4. **Notify Key Contacts:**
   - Use the radio to inform key contacts (e.g., family members) about the medical emergency and the steps being taken.
   - Keep them updated on the patient's status and any changes in the situation.

5. **Document and Communicate:**
   - Record vital information such as symptoms, time of onset, and any treatments administered.
   - Use the radio to relay this information to EMS personnel upon their arrival.

Search and Rescue Operations

Scenario: A member of your group or a hiker in your vicinity has gone missing, and a search and rescue operation is underway.

Objective: Coordinate search efforts, provide updates to rescue teams, and maintain safety protocols during the search.

Communication Plan:

1. Establish communication protocols with search and rescue teams on designated emergency channels.
2. Assign roles for coordinating search efforts, providing updates, and maintaining safety.

Steps:

1. **Initiate Search Protocol:**

   o Use the designated emergency channel to initiate the search protocol and coordinate efforts with other search team members.
   o Designate a central point of contact for relaying information to search teams.

2. **Assign Search Areas:**

   o Divide the search area into manageable sections and assign specific sections to different team members.
   o Use the radio to ensure clear communication and coordination among all search teams.

3. **Provide Updates:**

   o Regularly update the team on your progress and any findings.
   o Report any signs, tracks, or clues that could indicate the missing individual's location.

4. **Coordinate with Authorities:**

   o Maintain contact with local authorities or official search and rescue teams to synchronize efforts and share information.
   o Follow any instructions or guidance provided by official teams.

5. **Ensure Safety:**

   o Use the radio to maintain safety protocols, ensuring that all team members are accounted for and safe.

- Immediately report any injuries or hazards encountered during the search.

Community Coordination During Power Outages

Scenario: A severe storm has caused widespread power outages in your community, disrupting communication and access to essential services.

Objective: Maintain communication with community members, coordinate resources, and provide mutual assistance during the outage.

Communication Plan:

1. Establish a community communication network on designated emergency channels.
2. Compile a list of community contacts and assign roles for resource coordination and communication.

Steps:

1. **Establish a Community Network:**
   - Use Baofeng radios to establish a communication network with neighbors and community members.
   - Designate a primary channel for community communication and ensure that all members are aware of it.

2. **Coordinate Resources:**
   - Use the radio to coordinate the sharing of resources such as food, water, and medical supplies among community members.
   - Communicate needs and availability of resources within the community network to ensure equitable distribution.

3. **Provide Updates:**
   - Relay updates on the status of the power outage, estimated restoration times, and any emergency services information received.
   - Keep community members informed about safety tips, emergency procedures, and local developments.

4. **Offer Assistance:**
   - Use the radio to offer and coordinate assistance to those in need within the community.

- Organize volunteer efforts for tasks such as clearing debris, providing transportation, or checking on isolated neighbors.

5. **Maintain Morale:**

    - Use the radio to maintain morale by sharing positive news, encouraging messages, and coordinating social activities within the community.
    - Ensure regular communication to keep everyone connected and supported during the outage.

Coordination with Emergency Services

Scenario: A significant emergency, such as a large-scale fire or public safety incident, requires coordination with local emergency services for response and assistance.

Objective: Facilitate effective communication and coordination with emergency services to enhance response efforts and ensure public safety.

Communication Plan:

1. Establish contact with local emergency services on designated emergency channels and frequencies.
2. Designate roles for liaison with emergency services, reporting incidents, and relaying instructions to affected parties.

Steps:

1. **Establish Contact with Emergency Services:**

    - Use the designated emergency channel to establish initial contact with local emergency services (e.g., fire department, police, EMS).
    - Provide clear and concise information about the nature of the emergency, location, and any immediate threats.

2. **Provide Situation Reports:**

    - Continuously provide situation reports to emergency services, including updates on the incident, changes in conditions, and resource needs.
    - Relay information received from emergency services to affected parties to ensure public safety.

3. **Follow Instructions:**

- Follow instructions provided by emergency services personnel, including evacuation orders, shelter-in-place directives, or safety precautions.
- Ensure that all communication with emergency services is clear, accurate, and timely to facilitate an effective response.

4. **Assist with Coordination:**

    - Use your Baofeng radio to assist emergency services with coordination efforts, such as directing responders to specific locations or relaying information from the field to command centers.
    - Provide support as needed to ensure seamless communication and collaboration between response agencies.

5. **Report Updates and Changes:**

    - Continuously update emergency services on any changes in the situation, new hazards, or additional needs arising during the incident.
    - Ensure that all communication is documented and relayed promptly to facilitate informed decision-making by emergency services personnel.

Baofeng radios are powerful tools that can significantly enhance communication during emergencies. By creating an effective communication plan and understanding how to apply it in various scenarios, you can ensure that you and your community are prepared to respond effectively to any crisis.

Chapter 5:

Maintenance and Troubleshooting

Maintaining your Baofeng radio in good condition is essential to ensure reliable performance during critical situations. Regular maintenance prevents problems before they start and empowers you to detect and resolve any potential issues early. Moreover, mastering common troubleshooting techniques can spare you time and aggravation, guaranteeing that your radio is consistently operational when required. In this chapter, we'll discuss regular maintenance tips and troubleshooting common issues with Baofeng radios.

Regular Maintenance Tips

Regular maintenance helps keep your Baofeng radio in top condition and minimizes the risk of malfunctions. By incorporating these maintenance tips into your routine, you can prolong the life of your radio and ensure reliable performance when you need it most.

1. **Cleaning Your Radio**

Dust, dirt, and grime can accumulate on your radio over time, potentially affecting its performance and longevity. Regular cleaning helps prevent these contaminants from interfering with the radio's buttons, knobs, and ports.

Steps for Cleaning:

- **Exterior Cleaning**: To clean your Baofeng radio, opt for a soft, dry cloth to gently wipe its exterior surfaces. To prevent scratching or otherwise damaging the surface, you should steer clear of abrasive items and harsh chemicals.
- **Buttons and Knobs**: Pay special attention to the buttons and knobs. Use a small, soft brush to remove any dirt or debris that may have accumulated around them. For more stubborn dirt, a slightly damp cloth (with water only) can be used, but ensure no moisture seeps into the radio.
- **Ports and Connectors**: Inspect the ports and connectors, such as the antenna connector and charging port. Use a dry, soft-bristled brush to clean these areas carefully. If there is any visible dirt inside the ports, consider using a can of compressed air to blow it out gently.

Clean your radio at least once a month or more frequently if used in dusty or dirty environments.

2. **Inspecting the Antenna and Connections**

The antenna and its connection to the radio are crucial for effective communication. A damaged antenna or a poor connection can significantly degrade signal quality.

Steps for Inspection:

- **Visual Inspection**: Inspection of the antenna should be performed on a regular basis to look for any symptoms of physical degradation, like cracks, bends, or corrosion. A damaged antenna should be replaced immediately.
- **Connection Check**: Ensure that the antenna is securely attached to the radio. Loose connections can lead to poor transmission and reception quality. Tighten the antenna connector if necessary, but avoid over-tightening, which could strip the threads or damage the connector.
- **Connector Condition**: Examine the antenna connector for any signs of corrosion or dirt. Clean the connector using a dry cloth or a small brush. If corrosion is present, consider replacing the connector or the antenna.

Inspect the antenna and connections at least once a month or before each use if the radio is used infrequently.

3. **Checking and Maintaining the Battery**

The battery is the lifeline of your Baofeng radio. Proper battery maintenance ensures that your radio remains powered and ready for use.

Steps for Battery Maintenance:

- **Visual Inspection**: The battery should be inspected on a regular basis for any signs of wear, damage, or swelling. A damaged or swollen battery should be replaced immediately to prevent leaks or potential hazards.
- **Contact Cleaning**: You need to make sure that the contacts on the battery are clean and free of any corrosion. To clean the contacts in a gentle manner, you can use an eraser or a soft cloth. If you want to avoid damaging the contacts, you should avoid using abrasive materials.
- **Charging Practices**: Ensure that you charge the battery in accordance with the manufacturer's instructions. Because doing so will shorten the battery's lifespan, it is important to avoid overcharging it or regularly discharging it totally. Use only the recommended charger for your Baofeng radio.
- **Storage**: When you intend to put your radio away for a lengthy period of time, you should take out the battery and put it away in a separate location that is cold and dry. Battery drain and potential leakage are both prevented as a result of this.

Inspect and maintain the battery every month and before each use.

4. **Performing Functional Tests**

Regular functional tests ensure that all features of your Baofeng radio are working correctly. Identifying and addressing issues early can prevent failures during critical situations.

Steps for Functional Testing:

- **Basic Operation**: Turn on the radio and check if it powers up correctly. Ensure that the display, buttons, and knobs respond as expected.
- **Transmitting and Receiving**: Test the radio's ability to transmit and receive signals. Use a second radio or contact a nearby operator to perform this test. Ensure that your transmissions are clear and that you can receive incoming signals without issues.
- **Volume and Squelch**: Adjust the volume and squelch settings to ensure they work correctly. The volume should adjust smoothly, and the squelch should filter out background noise effectively.
- **Scanning and Channels**: Test the scanning feature to ensure it cycles through the channels correctly. Check that you can switch between channels and that each channel is programmed correctly.

Perform functional tests monthly and before each use, especially if the radio has been stored for a while.

5. **Updating Firmware and Software**

Importance of Updates: Keeping your radio's firmware and software up to date can improve performance, fix bugs, and introduce new features. It ensures that your radio operates with the latest enhancements and security measures.

Steps for Updating:

- **Check for Updates**: Regularly visit the manufacturer's website or support forums to check for firmware and software updates specific to your Baofeng model.
- **Download Updates**: Follow the instructions to download the latest updates. Ensure that you download updates from reputable sources to avoid corrupt or malicious files.
- **Install Updates**: Be sure to carefully adhere to the directions for installation that were provided by the manufacturer. Use the recommended software tools and cables to connect your radio to your computer for updating.
- **Verify Update**: After updating, verify that the radio functions correctly. Perform a functional test to ensure that all features are working as expected.

Check for updates every three to six months or whenever you encounter issues that might be resolved by an update.

6. **Proper Storage Practices**

Proper storage helps prevent damage and ensures that your radio remains in good condition when not in use.

Steps for Proper Storage:

- **Environment**: Put your radio in a location that is cool, dry, and out of the direct sunlight, as well as away from excessive temperatures and dampness. Avoid places like car trunks or attics that can experience temperature fluctuations.
- **Protection**: Use a protective case or pouch to prevent scratches, dust accumulation, and physical damage. Ensure the case provides adequate ventilation to avoid overheating.
- **Battery Storage**: If storing the radio for an extended period, remove the battery to prevent drain and potential leakage. Store the battery separately in a cool, dry place.
- **Antenna Care**: Store the radio with the antenna detached if possible to prevent strain on the antenna connector. Keep the antenna in a safe place where it won't get bent or damaged.

Always follow proper storage practices when the radio is not in use, especially for extended periods.

7. **Periodic Comprehensive Maintenance**

Periodic comprehensive maintenance ensures that all aspects of the radio are checked and maintained, preventing small issues from becoming major problems.

Steps for Comprehensive Maintenance:

- **Detailed Inspection**: Conduct a thorough visual inspection of the entire radio, including the case, buttons, knobs, antenna, and connectors. Look for signs of wear, damage, or anything unusual.
- **Internal Cleaning**: If comfortable and experienced, consider opening the radio for internal cleaning. This should be done cautiously and only if you are confident in your ability to reassemble the radio correctly. Use compressed air to blow out any dust and ensure internal components are clean.
- **Lubrication**: If any parts require lubrication (such as the volume knob), use a suitable electronic lubricant sparingly. Avoid over-lubricating as this can attract dust and dirt.
- **Firmware and Software Review**: Review the current firmware and software versions and compare them with the latest available updates. Update as necessary.
- **Accessory Check**: Inspect all accessories such as the charger, external microphone, and earpiece for wear and proper functionality. Replace any worn or damaged accessories.

Perform comprehensive maintenance every six months or annually, depending on the frequency of use and operating conditions.

Troubleshooting Common Issues

Despite regular maintenance, Baofeng radios may encounter occasional issues that require troubleshooting. Knowing how to identify and resolve common problems can help you quickly restore functionality and minimize downtime. Here are some common issues and troubleshooting steps:

1. **No Power**

If your Baofeng radio does not power on when you press the power button, try the following troubleshooting steps:

- Ensure the battery connections are securely attached and free from corrosion.
- Replace depleted batteries with fresh ones or recharge them as needed.

- Verify that the battery contacts are clean and making proper contact with the batteries.
- If using a battery pack, ensure that it is fully charged and properly installed.
- Check the power adapter or charging cable for any signs of damage or wear.

If the radio still does not power on after performing these steps, there may be an issue with the internal circuitry or power supply. For more diagnosis and repair, you should get in touch with the manufacturer or seek the assistance of a specialist.

2. **Poor Audio Quality**

If you experience poor audio quality during transmissions or receptions, try the following troubleshooting steps:

- Adjust the volume level to ensure it is set to an appropriate level for your environment.
- Check the antenna connection to ensure it is securely attached and properly aligned.
- Move to a location with better signal reception or adjust the squelch level to reduce background noise.
- If using an external microphone or headset, ensure that it is connected properly and functioning correctly.
- Test the radio with different frequencies or channels to determine if the issue is specific to a certain frequency range.
- Replace the speaker or headset if it shows signs of damage or wear.

If poor audio quality persists despite these troubleshooting steps, there may be an issue with the radio's internal components or settings. Consider resetting the radio to its factory defaults or seeking professional assistance for further diagnosis and repair.

3. **Programming Errors**

If you encounter errors or difficulties when programming your Baofeng radio, follow these troubleshooting steps:

- Double-check the programming cable connections to ensure they are securely attached to both the radio and the computer.
- Verify that the programming software is compatible with your Baofeng radio model and firmware version.
- Check the frequency and channel settings to ensure they are programmed correctly according to your preferences and local regulations.
- If encountering errors during programming, try disconnecting and reconnecting the programming cable, restarting the software, or rebooting the computer.

- Refer to the user manual or online resources for step-by-step programming instructions and troubleshooting tips specific to your Baofeng radio model.

If programming errors persist despite these troubleshooting steps, there may be an issue with the programming cable, software, or radio firmware. Contact the manufacturer or seek assistance from online forums or communities for further guidance.

4. **Signal Interference**

If you experience signal interference or disruptions during transmissions or receptions, try the following troubleshooting steps:

- Adjust the squelch level to filter out background noise and interference.
- Move to a location with better signal reception or away from sources of electromagnetic interference, such as electronic devices or power lines.
- Check the antenna connection and alignment to ensure optimal signal transmission and reception.
- Experiment with different frequencies or channels to find a clear, interference-free signal.
- If operating in a crowded or congested frequency band, consider using CTCSS/DCS tones to filter out unwanted transmissions.
- Install a ferrite bead or choke on the antenna cable to reduce electromagnetic interference.

If signal interference persists despite these troubleshooting steps, there may be environmental factors or external sources of interference affecting signal quality. Experiment with different operating locations or seek advice from experienced radio operators for further guidance.

5. **Display Issues**

If you encounter display issues such as flickering, dimness, or blank screens, try the following troubleshooting steps:

- Check the battery level to ensure it is not depleted, as low battery power may affect display brightness.
- Adjust the display contrast or backlight settings to improve visibility in different lighting conditions.
- Inspect the display screen for any signs of damage or wear, such as scratches or cracks.
- Clean the display screen using a soft, dry cloth to remove any dust or dirt that may obstruct visibility.
- Reset the radio to its factory defaults to restore default display settings and configurations.

- Update the radio's firmware to the latest version, as display issues may be addressed in newer firmware releases.

If display issues persist despite these troubleshooting steps, there may be an underlying hardware or software issue with the radio. For more diagnosis and repair, you should get in touch with the manufacturer or seek the assistance of a specialist.

6. **Overheating**

If your Baofeng radio becomes excessively hot during use, follow these troubleshooting steps:

- Ensure that the radio is not operating at high power for extended periods, as this can cause overheating.
- Check for obstructions around the ventilation areas of the radio and ensure proper airflow.
- Avoid using the radio in direct sunlight or in environments with high ambient temperatures.
- Reduce the transmission power level or take breaks between transmissions to allow the radio to cool down.
- If using an external power source, ensure that it is within the recommended voltage and current ratings for your radio.

If overheating persists despite these troubleshooting steps, there may be an issue with the radio's internal components or cooling system. For more diagnosis and repair, you should get in touch with the manufacturer or seek the assistance of a specialist.

7. **Button Malfunction**

If the buttons on your Baofeng radio are unresponsive or malfunctioning, try the following troubleshooting steps:

- Clean the keypad area with a soft, dry cloth to remove any dust or debris that may be causing the buttons to stick.
- Inspect the buttons for any signs of physical damage or wear and replace them if necessary.
- Perform a factory reset on the radio to restore default settings and resolve any software-related issues.
- Ensure that the radio's firmware is up to date, as firmware updates may address button responsiveness issues.

If button malfunctions persist despite these troubleshooting steps, there may be an issue with the radio's internal keypad circuitry. For more diagnosis and repair, you should get in touch with the manufacturer or seek the assistance of a specialist.

8. **Inconsistent Reception**

If your Baofeng radio has inconsistent reception, with signals cutting in and out, try the following troubleshooting steps:

- Check the antenna connection to ensure it is securely attached and properly aligned.
- Move to a location with fewer obstructions, such as buildings or trees, that may be blocking the signal.
- Adjust the squelch level to filter out weak signals and reduce background noise.
- Test the radio with different frequencies or channels to determine if the issue is specific to a certain frequency range.
- Replace the antenna with a higher-gain model to improve signal reception.

If inconsistent reception persists despite these troubleshooting steps, there may be environmental factors or external sources of interference affecting signal quality. Experiment with different operating locations or seek advice from experienced radio operators for further guidance.

Chapter 6:

Legal and Safety Considerations

When using Baofeng radios, it's crucial to adhere to legal regulations and practice safe usage to ensure effective and responsible communication. This chapter will provide a thorough overview of the legal and safety considerations you need to be aware of.

FCC Regulations and Legal Use

It is the responsibility of the FCC, which is the regulating authority, to control the utilization of radio frequencies in the United States. Understanding and adhering to FCC regulations is crucial for the legal operation of your Baofeng radio.

Licensing Requirements

To legally transmit on amateur radio frequencies using a Baofeng radio, you need an appropriate license from the FCC. There are three main classes of amateur radio licenses: Technician, General, and Amateur Extra. Each class offers different privileges and requires passing an exam.

1. **Technician License**: This is the entry-level license, allowing access to all VHF and UHF amateur bands (144-148 MHz and 420-450 MHz), which are commonly used by Baofeng radios. The Technician exam covers basic regulations, operating practices, and electronics theory.

2. **General License**: This intermediate license grants access to additional HF (high-frequency) bands, enabling long-distance communication. The General exam builds on the Technician material with more advanced concepts.

3. **Amateur Extra License**: The highest level of amateur radio licensing, the Amateur Extra license provides full access to all amateur bands and frequencies. The exam is the most challenging, covering extensive technical and regulatory knowledge.

How to Obtain a License:

- **Study Materials**: Utilize study guides, online resources, and practice exams from organizations like the American Radio Relay League (ARRL). There are numerous books, websites, and apps designed to help you prepare for the exams.
- **Exams**: Exams are administered by Volunteer Examiner Coordinators (VECs) across the country. Find a nearby exam session and register to take the test. VECs typically offer exams on a regular basis in many locations.
- **Fee**: The FCC charges a small fee for license applications and renewals.

Frequency Allocations

The FCC allocates specific frequency bands for different types of radio services. It's crucial to use the correct frequencies to avoid interference and ensure legal operation.

- **Amateur Bands**: Baofeng radios are primarily used on VHF (144-148 MHz) and UHF (420-450 MHz) amateur radio bands. These bands are allocated for non-commercial, personal, and emergency communications.
- **Public Safety and Commercial Bands**: Frequencies outside the amateur bands are often reserved for public safety, commercial, and government use. Unauthorized transmission on these frequencies can result in severe penalties.
- **Band Plans**: Each amateur radio band has a band plan, which is a voluntary guideline that specifies which frequencies are used for specific types of communication (e.g., voice, digital modes, CW). Following the band plan helps avoid interference with other users.

Power Limits

The FCC sets power limits to minimize interference and ensure safe operation.

- **Handheld Radios**: Baofeng handheld radios typically operate at a maximum power output of 5 watts. This is sufficient for most local communications within a few miles, especially when using repeaters.
- **Base Stations and Repeaters**: Higher power levels are permitted for fixed base stations and repeaters, but these setups require additional licensing and must adhere to more stringent regulations.
- **Effective Radiated Power (ERP)**: When calculating power limits, consider the Effective Radiated Power, which includes the transmitter power, antenna gain, and losses in the feedline. Ensuring your ERP is within legal limits is essential for compliance.

Permissible Communications

The FCC outlines what types of communications are allowed on amateur radio frequencies.

- **Personal Communications**: Licensed amateur operators can use their radios for personal, hobby-related communications. This includes casual conversations, technical discussions, and participation in amateur radio nets.
- **Emergency Communications**: In emergencies, amateur radio operators can use their equipment to provide critical communications when other means are unavailable. This is a key aspect of amateur radio's public service role. Emergency communications take priority over all other uses.
- **Non-Commercial**: All communications on amateur bands must be non-commercial. This means you cannot use your amateur radio for business purposes, including advertising or conducting business transactions.

Prohibited Communications

Certain types of communications are explicitly prohibited by the FCC to maintain the integrity of the amateur radio service.

- **Commercial Use**: Using amateur radio frequencies for business or commercial purposes is strictly forbidden. This includes any form of advertisement, sales, or business-related communication.
- **Obscene or Indecent Language**: Transmissions that contain obscene, indecent, or profane language are prohibited. Amateur radio operators are expected to maintain a high standard of conduct on the air.
- **Encryption**: Encrypting transmissions to obscure the content is generally not allowed, with limited exceptions for control signals to space stations or certain remote control operations. The content of amateur radio communications must be open and accessible to all.
- **False Distress Signals**: Transmitting false distress signals or causing willful interference to other communications is illegal and can result in severe penalties.

Frequency Coordination

To avoid interference and ensure efficient use of the spectrum, frequency coordination is essential.

- **Repeater Coordination**: Local amateur radio clubs and organizations often manage frequency coordination for repeaters. Using a coordinated frequency helps avoid conflicts with other repeaters and ensures reliable coverage. Coordinators keep track of active repeaters and assign frequencies to minimize interference.
- **Simplex Frequencies**: For direct communication without repeaters, use established simplex frequencies that are less likely to be congested. These are often listed in amateur radio band plans. Simplex operation is useful for short-range communication where repeaters are not needed.

- **Contacting a Frequency Coordinator**: If you plan to set up a new repeater or use a frequency for a significant event, contact your local frequency coordinator to ensure you are operating on a clear channel.

Interference Avoidance

Preventing and resolving interference is a critical aspect of legal and responsible radio operation.

- **Harmful Interference**: Operators must avoid causing harmful interference to other radio services. If notified of causing interference, operators are required to take immediate action to correct the issue. This might involve changing frequencies, reducing power, or modifying antenna setups.
- **Interference Resolution**: Work with local amateur radio clubs, the ARRL, and the FCC to resolve interference issues. This may involve adjusting frequencies, reducing power output, or using better antennas. Cooperation and communication with other users are key to resolving conflicts.
- **RFI Mitigation**: Radio Frequency Interference (RFI) can originate from various electronic devices. Using filters, proper grounding, and shielding can help mitigate RFI. Identifying and eliminating sources of RFI is part of responsible amateur radio operation.

Legal Use of Baofeng Radios

Legal operation of Baofeng radios involves understanding and complying with the above FCC regulations. Here's how to ensure you are using your radio legally:

1. **Get Licensed**: Pass the appropriate FCC exam and obtain your amateur radio license. Display your call sign on your radio and use it during all transmissions.

2. **Use Assigned Frequencies**: Only transmit on frequencies allocated for amateur radio use. Avoid public safety, commercial, and other restricted bands.

3. **Adhere to Power Limits**: Operate within the power limits specified by the FCC for handheld radios and other equipment.

4. **Permissible Communications**: Engage in personal, non-commercial communications and prioritize emergency traffic when necessary.

5. **Avoid Prohibited Communications**: Do not use your radio for commercial purposes, avoid obscene language, and do not encrypt your transmissions.

6. **Coordinate Frequencies**: Use repeaters and simplex frequencies that are coordinated and recommended by local amateur radio organizations.
7. **Prevent Interference**: Take steps to avoid causing interference and resolve any issues promptly if they arise.

FCC Enforcement and Penalties

The FCC actively monitors radio frequencies and enforces regulations to ensure compliance. Penalties for violating FCC rules can be severe and may include:

- **Fines**: Substantial monetary fines for illegal transmissions, interference, or operating without a license. The fines can vary depending on the severity and frequency of the violations.
- **License Revocation**: Suspension or revocation of your amateur radio license for repeated or serious violations. This means losing your privileges to operate on amateur frequencies.
- **Equipment Confiscation**: Seizure of radio equipment used in violation of FCC regulations. This can occur if the equipment is used to cause harmful interference or operate on unauthorized frequencies.
- **Criminal Charges**: In extreme cases, criminal charges may be filed for willful and malicious interference or other serious offenses. This can result in imprisonment and more severe penalties.

To avoid these penalties, always follow FCC regulations and operate your Baofeng radio responsibly. Regularly review the FCC rules and stay informed about any updates or changes.

Safety Tips for Radio Usage

Using Baofeng radios, or any other communication equipment, comes with certain safety considerations to ensure both the well-being of the operator and the effective operation of the device. This comprehensive guide will cover various safety tips and best practices to help you use your radio equipment safely and responsibly.

Electrical Safety

1. **Avoid Exposure to Moisture**: Electronic devices, including Baofeng radios, should be kept dry to prevent electrical shorts or damage. Avoid using the radio in heavy rain or submerging it in water. If your radio gets wet, turn it off immediately and let it dry completely before using it again.

2. **Use Proper Power Supplies**: When charging your Baofeng radio, always use the manufacturer-recommended power supplies and chargers. Utilizing an incompatible charger can lead to overcharging, overheating, or even explosions. It's crucial to verify that the voltage and current ratings align with the specifications of your radio to avoid these risks.

3. **Inspect Cables and Connectors**: Regularly check the power cables and connectors for signs of wear or damage. Frayed wires or damaged connectors can cause electrical shocks or fires. Replace any damaged components immediately.

4. **Prevent Overcharging**: Do not leave your Baofeng radio charging unattended for long periods. Overcharging poses a risk of battery damage and potential fire hazards. Whenever feasible, utilize a charger equipped with an automatic shut-off feature to mitigate this risk.

5. **Avoid DIY Repairs**: Unless you are trained and experienced in electronics repair, avoid attempting to fix your Baofeng radio yourself. Incorrect repairs can lead to electrical hazards. Instead, you should seek the advice of a technical expert or get in touch with the manufacturer to request support.

Handling and Operational Safety

1. **Proper Antenna Use**: Always attach an appropriate antenna before powering on your Baofeng radio. Operating the radio without an antenna, or with an improper antenna, can damage the radio's internal components and reduce transmission efficiency.

2. **Handling Batteries Safely**: Lithium-ion batteries, commonly used in Baofeng radios, require careful handling. Avoid puncturing or exposing the battery to high temperatures. Store spare batteries in a cool, dry place and avoid carrying them loose in pockets where they might short circuit.

3. **Mind Your Surroundings**: When using your Baofeng radio in outdoor environments, be aware of your surroundings to avoid accidents. For example, do not use the radio while driving unless you have a hands-free setup. Ensure that you are stationary and aware of your environment to prevent trips, falls, or other accidents.

4. **Secure Equipment Properly**: When operating in mobile settings, such as a vehicle, ensure that your radio and accessories are securely mounted. Loose equipment can become projectiles in the event of sudden stops or collisions.

Electromagnetic Field (EMF) Exposure

1. **Understand RF Exposure Limits**: The FCC sets limits on Radio Frequency (RF) exposure to protect users from excessive electromagnetic radiation. Familiarize yourself with these limits and ensure your radio use stays within safe levels.

2. **Maintain Safe Distances**: Keep the antenna at least several inches away from your body while transmitting. The higher the power output, the greater the distance should be. For handheld radios, using an external microphone can help maintain a safe distance.

3. **Avoid Prolonged Exposure**: Limit the duration of your transmissions to minimize RF exposure. Use short, efficient communication and avoid extended conversations on high power settings.

4. **Use Low Power Settings When Possible**: Operate your Baofeng radio on the lowest power setting that meets your communication needs. Lower power settings reduce RF exposure and conserve battery life.

Emergency Preparedness and Situational Awareness

1. **Know Emergency Protocols**: Familiarize yourself with emergency communication protocols and procedures. This includes understanding local emergency frequencies, call signs, and the correct format for distress calls.

2. **Regular Drills and Practice**: Conduct regular drills to practice your emergency communication plan. This helps ensure that you and your family or group know how to use the radios effectively in a real emergency.

3. **Backup Power Options**: Have backup power options available, such as spare batteries or a portable solar charger, to ensure your radio remains operational during extended emergencies.

4. **Stay Informed About Local Hazards**: Be aware of the specific hazards in your area, such as severe weather, earthquakes, or industrial accidents. Tailor your communication plan to address these specific risks.

General Safety Practices

1. **Regular Equipment Checks**: Perform regular checks of your Baofeng radio and accessories to ensure everything is in good working order. Check for signs of damage, wear, or malfunction, and address any issues promptly.

2. **Safe Storage**: When not being used, make sure to keep your Baofeng radio in a dry and cold location. Never keep the radio in situations that are either significantly hot or very chilly, as well as in direct sunlight, which can damage the internal components and battery.

3. **Training and Education**: Invest time in learning about amateur radio operation, safety practices, and emergency communication. Join local amateur radio clubs, participate in training sessions, and stay current with FCC regulations and best practices.

4. **Use of Protective Gear**: In certain environments, such as construction sites or disaster areas, wearing appropriate protective gear (e.g., helmets, gloves) can prevent physical injuries while using your radio.

Environmental Considerations

1. **Avoid Static Discharge**: Electricity that is static can cause damage to electrical components that are sensitive. Make sure to discharge any static energy that may be present by touching a grounded metal item before handling your Baofeng radio.

2. **Weather Conditions**: Be mindful of weather conditions that could affect radio performance or safety. For example, avoid using your radio during thunderstorms to prevent lightning strikes. Extreme temperatures can also impact battery life and radio performance.

3. **Interference Awareness**: Be aware of potential sources of interference in your surroundings, such as other electronic devices or industrial equipment. Interference can affect the performance of your radio and may pose a safety risk in critical communication scenarios.

4. **Disposal of Electronic Waste**: When it's time to dispose of old or damaged radio equipment, follow local regulations for electronic waste disposal. Proper disposal helps protect the environment and reduces the risk of hazardous materials contaminating the ecosystem.

Psychological and Social Considerations

1. **Stay Calm and Clear**: In emergency situations, it's important to stay calm and communicate clearly. Panic can lead to miscommunication and errors. Practice clear, concise communication techniques to ensure your messages are understood.

2. **Coordinate with Others**: Effective communication often involves coordinating with other radio users. Establish clear protocols for who will speak, in what order, and what information needs to be relayed. This reduces confusion and ensures important messages are prioritized.

3. **Respect Privacy and Security**: Be mindful of privacy and security when using your radio. Avoid sharing sensitive personal information over the airwaves. In certain situations, using coded language or agreed-upon signals can enhance security.

4. **Mental Preparedness**: Using a radio in high-stress situations requires mental preparedness. Regularly review your emergency communication plan and practice using your radio under simulated stress conditions to build confidence and proficiency.

When working with radio equipment such as Baofeng radios, safety ought to be the first concern whenever possible. By adhering to these safety guidelines and best practices, you can reduce the likelihood of being involved in an accident, protect yourself and others from harm, and ensure the reliable operation of your radio equipment. Remember to stay informed about relevant safety guidelines and regulations, and always use your radio equipment responsibly.

Chapter 7:

Enhancing Your Baofeng Experience

Your Baofeng radio is a versatile tool that can be customized and expanded to meet a wide range of communication needs. By investing in recommended accessories and exploring additional communication capabilities, you can enhance your Baofeng experience and unlock new possibilities for personal, professional, and emergency communication. This chapter will delve into various ways to optimize and expand your Baofeng radio setup, including the use of recommended accessories and techniques for expanding your communication capabilities.

Recommended Accessories

Whether you're using your radio for everyday communication, outdoor adventures, emergency preparedness, or professional applications, investing in the right accessories can significantly improve your user experience. In this comprehensive guide, we'll explore a variety of recommended accessories that can enhance your Baofeng radio setup and expand its capabilities.

1. **External Antennas**

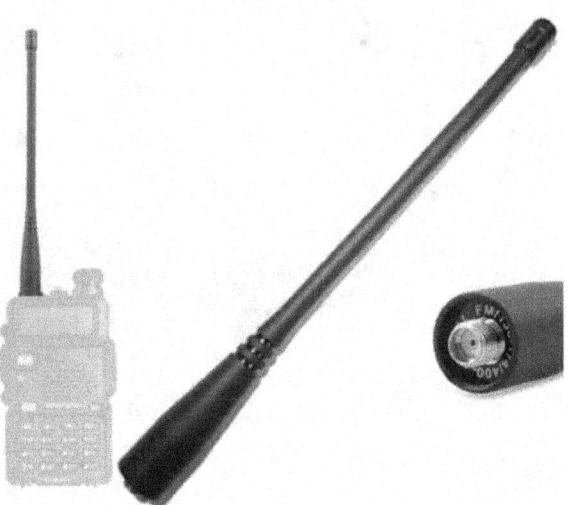

One of the most impactful accessories you can invest in for your Baofeng radio is an external antenna. While the stock antenna that comes with your radio may suffice for basic communication, upgrading to a high-quality external antenna can dramatically improve your radio's transmission and reception capabilities. External antennas are available in various designs, including whip antennas, dipole antennas, and Yagi antennas, each optimized for different frequency ranges and applications.

Benefits:

- **Improved Range**: External antennas typically offer higher gain and better radiation patterns than stock antennas, allowing for increased communication range and coverage.
- **Enhanced Signal Quality**: A well-designed external antenna can minimize signal distortion, interference, and multipath effects, resulting in clearer and more reliable communication.
- **Versatility**: External antennas can be mounted on vehicles, buildings, or portable masts, providing flexibility for mobile, base station, or field operations.
- **Customization**: External antennas come in various lengths, shapes, and configurations to suit different operating environments, frequencies, and user preferences.

2. **Headsets and Microphones**

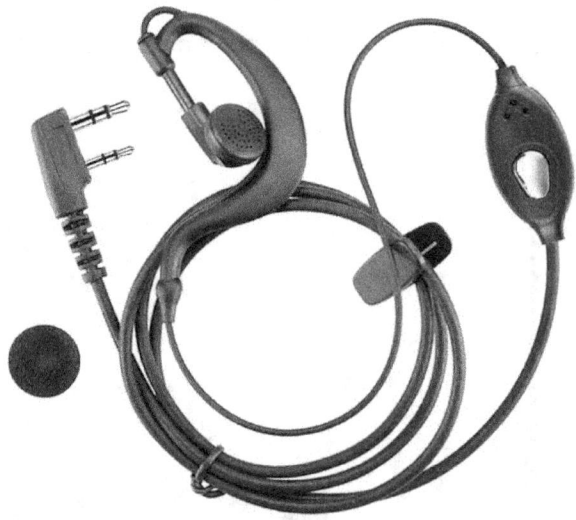

For hands-free operation and improved communication clarity, consider investing in a headset or microphone with a push-to-talk (PTT) button compatible with your Baofeng radio. Headsets and microphones are invaluable accessories for users who need to communicate while on the move, in noisy environments, or while performing other tasks. Choose a headset or microphone with adjustable volume, comfortable earpieces, and noise-canceling features for optimal performance.

Benefits:

- **Hands-Free Operation**: Headsets and microphones allow you to communicate without the need to hold the radio, freeing up your hands for other tasks or activities.
- **Noise Reduction**: Headsets with noise-canceling microphones can filter out background noise, making it easier to hear and understand incoming transmissions in noisy environments.
- **Privacy**: Using a headset or microphone with an earpiece ensures private communication by directing audio directly to your ears, minimizing the risk of eavesdropping.
- **Comfort**: High-quality headsets are designed for comfort during extended wear, with adjustable headbands, cushioned ear cups, and lightweight construction.

3. **Battery Packs and Chargers**

To ensure uninterrupted operation of your Baofeng radio, especially during extended outings or emergency situations, it's essential to have spare battery packs and reliable chargers on hand. Lithium-ion batteries, commonly used in Baofeng radios, provide high energy density and long-lasting performance but may require occasional replacement or recharging. Invest in high-capacity battery packs, portable power banks, or solar chargers to keep your radio powered up when off the grid.

Benefits:

- **Extended Runtime**: Spare battery packs allow you to swap out depleted batteries for fully charged ones, ensuring continuous operation of your Baofeng radio without interruption.
- **Versatility**: Portable power banks and solar chargers provide alternative power sources for recharging your radio's batteries in remote or off-grid locations where traditional power outlets may not be available.
- **Redundancy**: Having multiple charging options and backup power sources reduces the risk of running out of power during emergencies or prolonged outings.
- **Convenience**: Compact and lightweight chargers are easy to carry and can be used in a variety of settings, from outdoor adventures to vehicle installations.

4. **Carrying Cases and Holsters**

Protect your Baofeng radio from dust, moisture, and impacts with a durable carrying case or holster. Carrying cases are essential accessories for users who frequently transport their radios or operate in rugged outdoor environments. Look for cases with reinforced padding, weather-resistant materials, and secure closures to safeguard your radio from damage during storage or transportation.

Benefits:

- **Protection**: Carrying cases and holsters shield your Baofeng radio from scratches, bumps, and other hazards encountered during travel, outdoor activities, or field operations.
- **Organization**: Many carrying cases feature compartments or pockets for storing spare batteries, antennas, earpieces, and other accessories, keeping everything organized and easily accessible.
- **Portability**: Compact and lightweight carrying cases are designed for portability, allowing you to transport your radio securely while on the move.
- **Customization**: Carrying cases come in various sizes, styles, and colors to suit different Baofeng radio models and user preferences.

5. **Programming Cables and Software**

Programming cables and software enable you to customize your Baofeng radio's settings, channels, and frequencies with greater ease and precision than manual programming. These accessories are particularly useful for users with multiple radios or complex channel configurations, as they streamline the programming process and ensure accurate configuration settings. Invest in a quality programming cable and compatible software package to maximize the flexibility and usability of your Baofeng radio.

Benefits:

- **Efficiency**: Programming cables and software automate the process of programming your Baofeng radio, saving time and reducing the likelihood of programming errors.
- **Precision**: Software-based programming tools provide advanced features for fine-tuning channel parameters, setting radio options, and managing memory banks with precision control.
- **Flexibility**: Programming software allows you to create, edit, and save channel configurations, frequency lists, and radio profiles for different operating scenarios or user preferences.
- **Accessibility**: Many programming software packages offer user-friendly interfaces and intuitive controls, making it easy for novice users to customize their radios without extensive technical knowledge.

6. **External Speakers**

Enhance audio clarity and volume on your Baofeng radio with an external speaker designed for mobile or base station use. External speakers are valuable accessories for users operating in noisy environments, vehicles, or outdoor settings where ambient noise may interfere with clear communication. Choose a compact, weather-resistant speaker with high-quality audio output and compatible with your Baofeng radio for optimal performance.

Benefits:

- **Improved Audio Quality**: External speakers provide louder, clearer, and more natural-sounding audio reproduction compared to built-in radio speakers, enhancing communication clarity and intelligibility.
- **Noise Suppression**: High-quality external speakers feature noise-canceling technology to suppress background noise and improve signal-to-noise ratio, making it easier to hear incoming transmissions in noisy environments.
- **Versatility**: External speakers come in various sizes and configurations to suit different mounting options, installation preferences, and operating environments, from desktop setups to vehicle installations.
- **Durability**: Weather-resistant external speakers are designed for outdoor use, with rugged construction, sealed enclosures, and corrosion-resistant components to withstand harsh environmental conditions.

7. **GPS Modules**

For those who need enhanced situational awareness and navigation capabilities, integrating a GPS module with your Baofeng radio is a valuable upgrade. GPS modules enable location tracking, waypoint marking, and route planning, which are especially useful during outdoor activities like hiking, camping, and search-and-rescue operations.

Benefits:

- **Location Tracking**: GPS modules allow you to track your exact location and share coordinates with others, improving safety and coordination during group activities or emergency situations.
- **Navigation**: Use GPS for waypoint marking and route planning, helping you navigate unfamiliar terrain or retrace your steps in challenging environments.
- **Emergency Response**: In emergencies, GPS data can be crucial for rescue teams to locate you quickly and accurately.
- **Integration**: Some Baofeng radios support seamless integration with GPS modules, enabling real-time location data transmission and enhanced communication features.

8. **Signal Boosters and Amplifiers**

Signal boosters and amplifiers are essential for extending the range and improving the reliability of your Baofeng radio in areas with weak signal coverage or significant terrain obstacles. These devices amplify the power of your transmitted and received signals, ensuring clearer communication over longer distances.

Benefits:

- **Extended Range**: Boosters and amplifiers can significantly increase the effective communication range of your radio, allowing you to stay connected over greater distances.
- **Improved Signal Quality**: By amplifying weak signals, these devices enhance the clarity and reliability of your communications, reducing the chances of missed or garbled transmissions.
- **Versatility**: Suitable for use in various environments, from urban areas with signal interference to remote regions with sparse coverage.
- **Legal Compliance**: Ensure that the booster or amplifier you choose is compatible with your Baofeng radio and complies with FCC regulations to avoid legal issues.

9. **Car Mounts and Mobile Antennas**

For users who frequently operate their Baofeng radios from vehicles, car mounts and mobile antennas are indispensable accessories. These tools provide secure mounting options and improved signal performance while on the move, making mobile communication more reliable and convenient.

Benefits:

- **Secure Mounting**: Car mounts keep your radio stable and accessible while driving, preventing distractions and ensuring safe operation.
- **Enhanced Performance**: Mobile antennas, typically higher gain than handheld antennas, improve signal strength and range, making mobile communication more effective.
- **Flexibility**: Various mounting options are available, including magnetic mounts, trunk mounts, and roof mounts, allowing you to choose the best setup for your vehicle and usage.
- **Convenience**: Easily switch between mobile and handheld use by detaching the radio from the car mount, providing flexibility for different communication scenarios.

10. **Emergency Beacons and SOS Devices**

Adding emergency beacons and SOS devices to your Baofeng radio setup enhances your safety and preparedness during outdoor adventures or remote expeditions. These devices can send distress signals, alert rescuers, and provide vital information about your location and condition in emergencies.

Benefits:

- **Distress Signaling**: Emergency beacons can transmit distress signals on specific frequencies, alerting rescuers to your location and situation.
- **Automatic Activation**: Many SOS devices are designed to activate automatically upon impact or submersion, ensuring timely assistance even if you are incapacitated.
- **Long Battery Life**: Designed for emergency use, these devices often have long battery life, ensuring they remain operational when needed.
- **Enhanced Safety**: Carrying an emergency beacon or SOS device provides peace of mind, knowing that you have a reliable means of calling for help in critical situations.

11. External Power Supplies

External power supplies, such as solar panels and portable generators, ensure that your Baofeng radio remains operational during extended outings or power outages. These accessories are particularly valuable for users who operate in remote areas or disaster-prone regions where access to electricity may be limited.

Benefits:

- **Continuous Operation**: External power supplies keep your radio and other essential devices powered up, ensuring uninterrupted communication and functionality.
- **Portability**: Portable power solutions like solar panels and compact generators are designed for easy transport and setup, making them ideal for outdoor activities and emergency preparedness.
- **Sustainability**: Solar panels provide a renewable energy source, reducing your reliance on disposable batteries and minimizing environmental impact.
- **Versatility**: External power supplies can be used to charge multiple devices, including radios, smartphones, and other electronic equipment, enhancing overall preparedness and convenience.

12. Additional Antenna Adapters and Connectors

To maximize the versatility of your Baofeng radio, consider investing in a variety of antenna adapters and connectors. These accessories allow you to connect different types of antennas and external devices, expanding your radio's capabilities and compatibility.

Benefits:

- **Compatibility**: Adapters and connectors enable you to use a wide range of antennas and accessories with your Baofeng radio, ensuring you can optimize your setup for different scenarios.

- **Flexibility**: Easily switch between different antennas and devices without modifying your radio, providing flexibility for various communication needs.
- **Enhanced Performance**: By using the appropriate adapters and connectors, you can ensure optimal signal transmission and reception, improving overall communication quality.
- **Convenience**: Having a selection of adapters and connectors on hand allows you to quickly and easily adapt your radio setup to changing conditions or requirements.

13. **Protective Skins and Covers**

Protective skins and covers help safeguard your Baofeng radio from physical damage, such as scratches, impacts, and environmental exposure. These accessories are especially useful for users who frequently operate in rugged or harsh environments.

Benefits:

- **Physical Protection**: Skins and covers shield your radio from damage caused by drops, bumps, and abrasive surfaces, extending its lifespan and maintaining its appearance.
- **Weather Resistance**: Many protective covers offer additional weather resistance, protecting your radio from dust, moisture, and extreme temperatures.
- **Customization**: Protective skins come in various colors and designs, allowing you to personalize your radio and make it easily identifiable.
- **Enhanced Grip**: Textured skins and covers provide a better grip, reducing the likelihood of accidental drops and improving handling in wet or slippery conditions.

Expanding Your Communication Capabilities

To fully utilize the potential of your Baofeng radio, it's essential to explore and expand its communication capabilities. Whether you're seeking to extend your range, improve signal quality, or integrate with different communication systems, enhancing your Baofeng setup can significantly broaden your operational scope. This section will delve into various techniques and tools to expand your communication capabilities, ensuring you get the most out of your Baofeng radio.

Cross-Band Repeating

Cross-band repeating is a powerful feature that allows your radio to retransmit signals received on one frequency to another frequency. This effectively extends your communication range and coverage area, making it particularly useful in situations where direct communication is not possible due to distance or obstructions.

Benefits:

- **Extended Range**: Cross-band repeating can significantly increase the effective communication range, allowing you to maintain contact over larger areas.
- **Improved Coverage**: This feature helps overcome obstacles such as buildings, terrain, or other physical barriers that can block direct signals.
- **Flexibility**: It enables communication between different frequency bands, allowing for more versatile and adaptable communication setups.

Setting Up Cross-Band Repeating:

1. **Select Compatible Radios**: Ensure that both your Baofeng radio and the secondary radio support cross-band repeating.

2. **Program Frequencies**: Program the input and output frequencies for each radio, ensuring they match the desired repeat configuration.

3. **Configure Repeater Settings**: Adjust the repeater settings on your Baofeng radio, such as squelch levels, time-out timers, and power levels.

4. **Test the Setup**: Conduct a series of tests to verify that the cross-band repeating is functioning correctly and that signals are being transmitted and received as expected.

Digital Modes and APRS

Digital communication modes offer advanced features and improved performance over traditional analog FM. Modes such as Digital Mobile Radio (DMR), System Fusion (C4FM), and Automatic Packet Reporting System (APRS) provide enhanced audio quality, data transmission capabilities, and network connectivity.

Benefits:

- **Clearer Audio**: Digital modes offer superior audio clarity and reduced background noise compared to analog FM.
- **Data Transmission**: Digital modes enable the transmission of text messages, images, and other data, expanding the functionality of your communication setup.
- **Networking**: Digital networks allow for advanced features like talk groups, GPS tracking, and real-time data sharing.

Implementing Digital Modes:

1. **Choose a Digital Mode**: Select the digital mode that best suits your needs (e.g., DMR, C4FM, APRS).
2. **Equip Your Radio**: Ensure your Baofeng radio supports the chosen digital mode or consider using a digital interface device.
3. **Program Channels**: Program the necessary channels and settings for digital communication, including talk groups and network IDs.
4. **Test and Practice**: Conduct tests to familiarize yourself with the digital mode features and ensure everything is functioning properly.

Satellite Communication

Satellite communication provides global coverage, enabling long-distance communication in areas where traditional radio signals cannot reach. Using handheld satellite transceivers or portable satellite antennas, you can establish reliable communication links regardless of your location.

Benefits:

- **Global Coverage**: Satellite communication offers worldwide coverage, ensuring connectivity even in the most remote locations.
- **Reliable**: Satellites provide consistent and reliable communication, unaffected by terrestrial obstacles or interference.

- **Emergency Use**: Satellite communication is invaluable in emergencies, providing a lifeline when other communication methods fail.

Setting Up Satellite Communication:

1. **Select a Satellite Device**: Choose a satellite transceiver or antenna compatible with your communication needs and budget.

2. **Activate Service**: Subscribe to a satellite communication service plan that provides the necessary coverage and features.

3. **Integrate with Baofeng**: Connect your Baofeng radio to the satellite device, if applicable, using the appropriate interface or adapter.

4. **Test Communication**: Perform tests to ensure the satellite setup is working correctly and that you can transmit and receive signals effectively.

Mesh Networking

Mesh networking allows radio nodes to dynamically connect and communicate with each other, forming ad hoc networks without relying on centralized infrastructure. This technology is ideal for creating resilient communication networks for emergency response, community events, or large-scale outdoor activities.

Benefits:

- **Resilience**: Mesh networks are self-healing and adaptive, automatically rerouting signals to maintain connectivity even if some nodes fail.
- **Scalability**: Mesh networks can scale to accommodate many users and devices, making them suitable for various applications.
- **Flexibility**: These networks can be rapidly deployed and reconfigured to meet changing communication needs.

Implementing Mesh Networking:

1. **Choose Mesh Protocol**: Select a mesh networking protocol compatible with your Baofeng radio, such as AREDN (Amateur Radio Emergency Data Network).

2. **Equip Radios**: Ensure your radios are equipped with the necessary hardware and software to support mesh networking.

3. **Configure Network**: Set up the mesh network by configuring each node's settings, including frequency, power, and network ID.

4. **Test and Deploy**: Test the mesh network to ensure all nodes are communicating effectively and deploy the network as needed.

Community Repeaters and Nets

Joining local amateur radio clubs, repeater groups, and emergency response networks can greatly expand your communication capabilities. Community repeaters and scheduled nets provide access to a wider range of frequencies, coordinated communication channels, and valuable support resources.

Benefits:

- **Extended Reach**: Community repeaters extend the communication range beyond what is possible with simplex operation.
- **Coordination**: Scheduled nets provide structured communication opportunities for training, information sharing, and emergency response.
- **Support**: Being part of a community offers access to experienced operators, technical assistance, and shared resources.

Participating in Community Repeaters and Nets:

1. **Find Local Groups**: Research and join local amateur radio clubs, repeater groups, and emergency response organizations.

2. **Program Frequencies**: Program the relevant repeater frequencies, tones, and offsets into your Baofeng radio.

3. **Participate Regularly**: Join scheduled nets and participate in community events to build relationships and improve your communication skills.

4. **Volunteer**: Offer your time and expertise to support community initiatives, emergency drills, and public service events.

Remote Control and Automation

Leveraging remote control and automation capabilities allows you to operate your Baofeng radio remotely from a computer, smartphone, or dedicated control panel. This can be particularly useful for base stations, mobile installations, or situations where direct access to the radio is not feasible.

Benefits:

- **Convenience**: Remote control provides the ability to operate your radio from a distance, making it easier to manage communications in various scenarios.
- **Advanced Features**: Remote control software often includes features such as frequency scanning, channel hopping, and telemetry monitoring.
- **Flexibility**: Automating certain radio functions can improve efficiency and reduce the need for manual intervention.

Implementing Remote Control and Automation:

1. **Choose Remote Control Software**: Select a software package compatible with your Baofeng radio and communication needs.

2. **Connect Radio**: Establish a connection between your radio and the remote control interface, typically via a programming cable or wireless adapter.

3. **Configure Settings**: Set up the remote control software, configuring settings for frequency control, audio routing, and other parameters.

4. **Test Functionality**: Conduct tests to ensure the remote control setup is working correctly and that you can effectively manage your radio remotely.

Interoperability and Cross-Band Operation

Establishing interoperable communication links between different radio systems, bands, and protocols is essential for seamless coordination across multiple user groups and agencies. Cross-band operation enables Baofeng radios to communicate with other radio types, including commercial, public safety, and military radios.

Benefits:

- **Seamless Coordination**: Interoperable communication links facilitate smooth coordination between different user groups and agencies.
- **Flexibility**: Cross-band operation allows you to switch between different frequency bands and modes as needed, adapting to various communication requirements.
- **Enhanced Capability**: Integrating with other radio systems expands your communication options and ensures compatibility with diverse equipment.

Implementing Interoperability and Cross-Band Operation:

1. **Identify Requirements**: Determine the interoperability requirements based on the user groups and communication systems involved.

2. **Select Compatible Equipment**: Ensure your Baofeng radio and any additional equipment support the necessary frequency bands and modes for interoperability.

3. **Program Channels**: Program the relevant frequencies, tones, and settings for cross-band operation and interoperability.

4. **Test and Verify**: Conduct tests to verify that the interoperability setup works as intended and that communication links are reliable and clear.

Emergency Preparedness and Public Service

Volunteering for public service events, community service projects, and emergency response activities can provide practical experience and contribute to the welfare of your community. Participation in these activities enhances your communication skills, teamwork, and readiness to assist in times of need.

Benefits:

- **Experience**: Hands-on participation in public service and emergency response activities provides valuable experience and improves your communication skills.
- **Community Contribution**: Volunteering supports your community, providing essential services and building resilience in times of crisis.
- **Readiness**: Regular involvement in drills, exercises, and events ensures you are well-prepared to respond effectively during actual emergencies.

Getting Involved in Emergency Preparedness and Public Service:

1. **Join Organizations**: Become a member of amateur radio emergency service groups, such as ARES (Amateur Radio Emergency Service) or RACES (Radio Amateur Civil Emergency Service).

2. **Participate in Drills**: Engage in regular emergency drills and exercises to practice your skills and improve coordination with other volunteers.

3. **Support Events**: Volunteer for public service events, such as marathons, parades, and community fairs, providing communication support and ensuring event safety.

4. **Stay Informed**: Keep up-to-date with emergency response protocols, local hazards, and community needs to remain ready and informed.

Remote Operation and Remote Control

Remote operation and control of your Baofeng radio allow for flexibility and convenience, enabling you to manage your communication system from a distance. This capability is particularly useful for base stations, repeater setups, and remote monitoring applications.

Benefits:

- **Flexibility**: Remote operation allows you to control your Baofeng radio from anywhere with an internet connection, offering flexibility and convenience.
- **Accessibility**: Remote control software and applications provide access to advanced radio features and functions that may not be available on the radio's physical interface.
- **Monitoring**: Remote monitoring enables you to keep track of your communication system's status, performance, and activity in real-time.
- **Automation**: Remote control interfaces often support automation features, allowing you to schedule tasks, activate macros, and streamline operations.

Implementing Remote Operation and Control:

1. **Choose Remote Control Software**: Select a remote control software or application compatible with your Baofeng radio model and communication requirements.

2. **Set Up Remote Access**: Configure remote access settings on your radio, including network connectivity options, security protocols, and authentication methods.

3. **Install and Configure Software**: Install the remote control software on your computer, smartphone, or tablet, and configure it to communicate with your radio.

4. **Test and Troubleshoot**: Conduct tests to verify remote operation and control functionality, ensuring that you can access and manage your radio remotely without issues.

Integration with Digital Voice Networks

Integrating your Baofeng radio with digital voice networks, such as DMR (Digital Mobile Radio) or D-STAR (Digital Smart Technologies for Amateur Radio), expands your communication options and provides access to advanced features and services.

Benefits:

- **Enhanced Audio Quality**: Digital voice networks offer superior audio quality and clarity compared to traditional analog FM, ensuring clear and intelligible communication.
- **Extended Coverage**: Digital voice networks often provide wider coverage and improved signal propagation, enabling communication over greater distances and in challenging environments.
- **Advanced Features**: Digital voice networks support features such as text messaging, GPS tracking, and group calls, enhancing communication capabilities and versatility.
- **Interoperability**: Many digital voice networks support cross-network communication, allowing users on different systems to communicate with each other seamlessly.

Integrating with Digital Voice Networks:

1. **Select Compatible Network**: Choose a digital voice network that aligns with your communication needs and preferences, such as DMR, D-STAR, or Fusion.

2. **Acquire Necessary Equipment**: Ensure your Baofeng radio is compatible with the chosen network or invest in additional equipment, such as a hotspot or repeater, if required.

3. **Configure Settings**: Program your radio with the necessary digital voice settings, including talk groups, reflectors, and access codes, to connect to the network.

4. **Connect and Communicate**: Establish a connection to the digital voice network and start communicating with other users, exploring the various features and capabilities available.

Packet Radio and APRS

Packet radio and Automatic Packet Reporting System (APRS) offer digital data communication capabilities over amateur radio frequencies, enabling messaging, telemetry, and position tracking.

Benefits:

- **Data Transmission**: Packet radio and APRS enable the transmission of text messages, telemetry data, and GPS coordinates, expanding communication beyond voice.
- **Position Tracking**: APRS provides real-time tracking of stations' positions, allowing for location-based services and situational awareness.
- **Emergency Reporting**: APRS can be used to send emergency beacons and distress messages, providing a valuable tool for search and rescue operations.
- **Network Integration**: Packet radio and APRS integrate with existing digital voice networks, repeaters, and internet gateways, enhancing interoperability and connectivity.

Implementing Packet Radio and APRS:

1. **Set Up TNC**: If using packet radio, connect a Terminal Node Controller (TNC) to your Baofeng radio to encode and decode packet data.

2. **Configure APRS Settings**: Program your radio with the necessary APRS settings, including your call sign, beacon interval, and digipeater paths.

3. **Connect to APRS Network**: Establish a connection to the APRS network by tuning to the appropriate frequency and configuring your radio for APRS operation.

4. **Transmit and Monitor**: Start transmitting APRS packets and monitoring the APRS network for incoming messages, beacons, and position reports.

Weather Monitoring and Alerting

Integrating your Baofeng radio with weather monitoring and alerting systems enables you to receive timely updates and warnings about severe weather events, natural disasters, and emergency situations.

Benefits:

- **Early Warning**: Weather monitoring systems provide early warning of severe weather events, giving you time to take appropriate precautions and respond accordingly.
- **Situational Awareness**: Real-time weather updates and alerts enhance situational awareness, helping you make informed decisions and stay safe during adverse conditions.
- **Emergency Preparedness**: Weather monitoring and alerting systems are essential components of emergency preparedness plans, ensuring you are ready to respond to weather-related emergencies.

Integrating with Weather Monitoring Systems:

1. **Program NOAA Weather Channels**: Program NOAA Weather Radio channels into your Baofeng radio to receive broadcasts from local weather stations.

2. **Enable Weather Alert Feature**: Activate the weather alert feature on your radio to receive automatic alerts for severe weather warnings and watches in your area.

3. **Connect to Weather Networks**: Integrate your radio with online weather networks and services, such as Weather Underground or Spotter Network, to access additional weather data and alerts.

4. **Stay Informed**: Monitor weather updates and alerts regularly, paying attention to changing conditions and taking appropriate action to ensure your safety and well-being.

By incorporating these advanced communication techniques and technologies into your Baofeng radio setup, you can expand your communication capabilities and enhance your ability to stay connected, informed, and prepared in a wide range of scenarios.

Conclusion

Congratulations on completing your journey to mastering the use of Baofeng radios and expanding your communication capabilities! Throughout this guide, we've explored a wide range of topics, from basic setup and programming to advanced features and applications. By now, you should feel confident in your ability to use your Baofeng radio effectively in various scenarios, whether for emergency communication, outdoor adventures, or amateur radio operations.

Recap of Key Points

Throughout this journey, we've covered a wide range of topics to help you unlock the full potential of your Baofeng radio:

- **Basic Setup and Operation**: We started by covering the essentials of setting up and operating your Baofeng radio, including unboxing, programming, and understanding basic functions. By mastering these fundamentals, you've laid a solid foundation for effective communication in various scenarios.
- **Advanced Features and Functions**: We delved into advanced features such as VOX, dual watch, repeater access, and scanning capabilities, empowering you to optimize your radio for enhanced performance and versatility. Understanding these features allows you to tailor your communication setup to meet specific needs and challenges.
- **Practical Applications and Scenarios**: We explored practical applications of Baofeng radios in emergency situations, outdoor adventures, and community service activities. By creating effective communication plans and scenario-based guides, you're better prepared to handle real-world challenges and ensure your safety and connectivity when it matters most.
- **Maintenance and Troubleshooting**: We discussed the importance of regular maintenance and troubleshooting to keep your radio in optimal condition and address common issues. By following maintenance tips and troubleshooting guidelines, you can prolong the lifespan of your equipment and maintain reliable communication capabilities.
- **Legal and Safety Considerations**: We highlighted the importance of understanding FCC regulations and safety tips for radio usage to ensure legal compliance and promote safe operating practices. By adhering to these regulations and guidelines, you can enjoy radio communication responsibly while minimizing risks and ensuring the well-being of yourself and others.

- **Enhancing Your Baofeng Experience**: We explored recommended accessories and techniques for expanding your communication capabilities, including GPS modules, signal boosters, satellite communication, and integration with digital voice networks. By incorporating these enhancements into your setup, you can maximize the potential of your Baofeng radio and adapt to a wide range of communication scenarios.

Continuing Your Journey in Radio Communication

Your journey in radio communication doesn't end here—it's just the beginning. As you continue to explore the world of Baofeng radios and amateur radio operation, consider the following steps to further enhance your skills and knowledge:

- **Join Amateur Radio Clubs**: Connect with fellow radio enthusiasts and amateur radio operators by joining local or online amateur radio clubs. Participating in club activities, events, and nets can provide valuable learning opportunities and foster a sense of community.
- **Attend Training and Workshops**: Take advantage of training sessions, workshops, and certification courses offered by amateur radio organizations and institutions. These resources can help you deepen your understanding of radio communication principles and techniques.
- **Participate in Public Service Events**: Volunteer for public service events, emergency drills, and community service projects that involve radio communication support. Engaging in public service activities not only contributes to the welfare of your community but also allows you to apply your radio skills in real-world scenarios.
- **Experiment and Innovate**: Don't be afraid to experiment with different antennas, modes, and communication setups to discover what works best for you. Embrace innovation and creativity in exploring new ways to leverage Baofeng radios for communication purposes.
- **Stay Informed**: Stay up-to-date with developments in the field of amateur radio, including advancements in technology, regulatory changes, and best practices. Follow reputable sources, such as amateur radio publications, online forums, and regulatory agencies, to stay informed and engaged.

By continuing your journey in radio communication and staying proactive in learning and exploring new possibilities, you'll further hone your skills, expand your knowledge, and contribute to the vibrant amateur radio community. Whether you're communicating for emergency preparedness, recreation, or community service, your commitment to excellence in radio communication will make a positive impact on those around you. Keep exploring, keep learning, and keep communicating—it's an exciting journey ahead.

www.ingramcontent.com/pod-product-compliance
Lightning Source LLC
Chambersburg PA
CBHW082238220526
45479CB00005B/1273